FIND YOUR FIERCE

HOW TO PUT SOCIAL ANXIETY IN ITS PLACE

By Jacqueline Sperling, PhD

Illustrated by Anya Kuvarzina

Magination Press · Washington, DC · American Psychological Association

I dedicate this book to the courageous readers
willing to look within to find their fierce. You're
among the bravest—*JS*

To John, who inspired me to become a designer—*AK*

**Books for Kids From the
American Psychological Association**
maginationpress.org

Text copyright © 2021 by Magination Press, an imprint of the American
Psychological Association. Illustrations copyright © 2021 by Anya Kuvarzina.
All rights reserved. Except as permitted under the United States Copyright Act
of 1976, no part of this publication may be reproduced or distributed in any form
or by any means, or stored in a database or retrieval system, without the prior
written permission of the publisher.

Magination Press is a registered trademark of the American Psychological
Association. Order books at maginationpress.org, or call 1-800-374-2721.

Book design by Rachel Ross
Cover printed by Phoenix Color, Hagerstown, MD
Interior printed by Sheridan Sheridan Books, Inc., Chelsea, MI

Cataloging-in-Publication Data is on file at the Library of Congress.

ISBN: 978-1-4338-3362-5 (hardcover)

Manufactured in the United States of America
10 9 8 7 6 5 4 3 2 1

TABLE OF CONTENTS

INTRODUCTION

You might have picked up this book because you feel extra worried about what others think of you, you find it challenging to talk to others you don't know well, or you feel uncomfortable in social situations. Whatever the reason, you're reading this book because you want to do something about it. That's impressive and takes a lot of courage.

Humans are supposed to care about what others think of them, and this starts feeling especially important when you're a teenager. That concern about what others think can sometimes turn into worry about being judged or embarrassed in front of others, grow even bigger, and get in the way of spending time with friends, participating in school, and going out in public. If that sounds like you, you might have social anxiety disorder and you most certainly would not be alone. Social anxiety disorder is the second most common anxiety disorder and affects many of your peers—over 9%. If there were 400 students in your school, that would mean that about 36 have social anxiety disorder. It may seem like you're the only one feeling this way, but you have a lot of company.

A lot of people with social anxiety disorder blame themselves for what they're experiencing. No one chooses to feel this way, though, and you certainly did not sign yourself up for this. You might have inherited some genes that make you more likely to experience social anxiety—a lot of teens with social anxiety also have a parent with social anxiety. Sometimes stressful events or big life changes, such as moving to a new school, being bullied, or going through puberty, can bring your social anxiety front and center. You didn't choose this, but you can do something about it by applying the skills you'll learn in this book.

People with social anxiety disorder often think that they're not likable or that they can't do anything well. This couldn't be farther from the truth, but teens might feel this way because they have yet to discover that their social anxiety can actually be a blessing in disguise. Imagine those around you were given an average car to drive, but you were given a sports car. The sports car has a sensitive engine. You gently tap the gas pedal, and the car may jolt forward and yank you around. You have to learn how to drive this car in a way that maximizes, or gets the most out of, all its impressive skills. No one is born knowing how to drive the car; you have to learn the skills and practice them to make that happen.

How does this apply to your anxiety? Your anxiety likely makes you very aware of how others are behaving and expressing feelings (this is your sensitive engine). This can be a gift! Sometimes, however, it can make you feel worried about how other people see you and you want to withdraw or pull back. That would be like parking your car, but staying put doesn't help you go where you want and need to go. Treat this book like an owner's manual to help you learn how to drive your sports car, instead of having the car drive you or keeping you parked. Once you finish training this gift of yours that can pick up on subtle signals, you may be even better at navigating social interactions and even more compassionate than some of your peers.

The skills in this book will build on each other as they go. When you learn a skill in one chapter, keep practicing that one while you move on to the next chapter—the combination of all these skills will help you take steps forward.

First, we'll go over what social anxiety and the treatments for it are. Second, we will walk through the role anxiety plays, and third, you will learn specific strategies, like how to boss worries back, relax your body, and train the brain to help you gradually get back to doing more of what you love to do. There will be activities throughout the book to help you practice your skills. You also will learn tools to manage anxiety in the future and keep it from managing you. You already are the expert on you, and hopefully this book will help you learn how to find your inner fierce to keep the social anxiety in check. Let's get started!

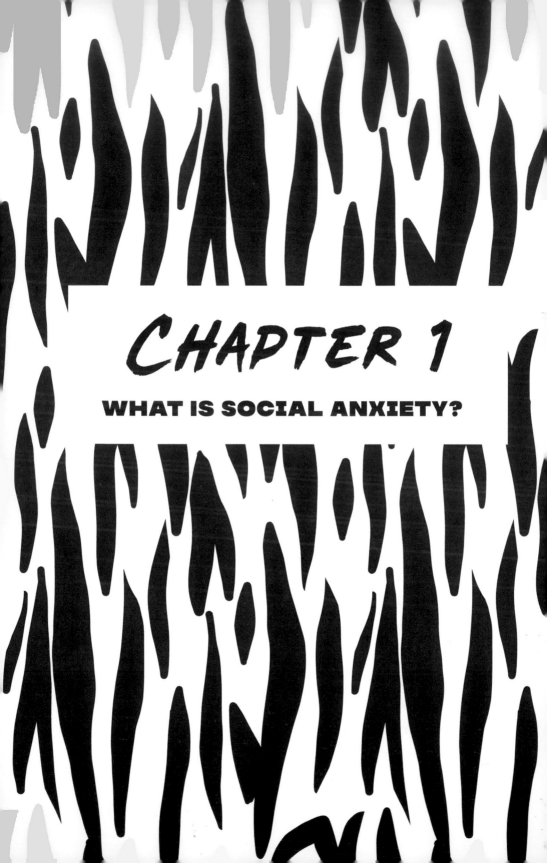

CHAPTER 1

WHAT IS SOCIAL ANXIETY?

What exactly is social anxiety disorder? It's formally defined as a fear of judgment or embarrassment that has lasted for at least six months and gets in the way of life at home, at school, or in other social environments. For example, social anxiety may make it difficult to attend family gatherings, complete homework, and spend time with friends. Those with social anxiety disorder may avoid raising their hands in class, going to parties, ordering in restaurants, making eye contact, giving a presentation, using public restrooms, eating in front of others, going to school, making phone calls, or texting friends. Social anxiety disorder can look different from one person to the next—coming up, you'll see a few examples of teens who have social anxiety disorder. Throughout the book, we'll see how these teens experience social anxiety, and there will be opportunities for you to practice what you've learned by thinking about their situations.

EMMA is a 16-year-old who worries that she will embarrass herself when she is in social settings. Emma avoids ordering in restaurants, seeking help from teachers, raising her hand in class, eating in the cafeteria, and asking people questions. Emma only eats meals at home because she worries about calling attention to herself and that people will think she is a slob for the way she eats. Emma's grades have gone down because she has not participated in class or received extra help from a teacher when she needed it. Although she is a talented actress and singer, she has not auditioned for the annual school play because she worries about messing up on stage. Emma also has turned down dates to school dances because she worries about dancing awkwardly in front of others.

JORDAN is a 15-year-old who worries about performing poorly in front of others. He thinks that if he participated in an activity, people would see him as pathetic and incapable of doing anything well. As a result, Jordan has stopped attending soccer practices and games. Jordan also quit playing the piano to avoid judgment and disappointment from his teacher at recitals. Jordan rarely raises his hand in class when he is unsure of the answer and skips school on days when he might have to work in a group or give a speech in front of his classmates. Jordan will have to take summer school classes to make up for the days he has missed due to his anxiety.

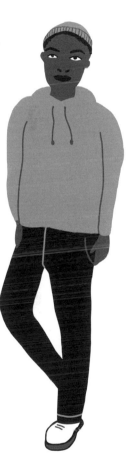

MARIA is a 13-year-old who worries about talking to her peers and trying to make new friends because she fears rejection and thinks she is unlikable. Maria avoids making eye contact and starting conversations, especially with people she does not know well. She believes that her one friend, Sophie, is only friends with her right now because she feels sorry for her and that Sophie might stop being her friend at any moment. Maria doesn't like texting with Sophie because she worries that her messages could be misunderstood. When talking to Sophie at school, Maria will agree with everything Sophie says and pretend to like everything Sophie enjoys because she worries that having a different opinion will make Sophie not want to spend time with her. Maria also avoids public places where she might run into her peers. She turns down birthday party invitations and won't go to malls, movie theaters, or the local town center.

Although social anxiety disorder can get in the way of everyday life, it can be managed with some skills. The aim of this book is to give you a toolbox so that you, and not your anxiety, can be the boss of you. Along with Emma, Jordan, and Maria, you will learn how to put your social anxiety in its place.

COGNITIVE BEHAVIORAL THERAPY (CBT)

Now that you've learned more about what social anxiety disorder is, you may be wondering what you can do about it. A type of treatment called cognitive behavioral therapy (CBT) with exposure and response prevention (ERP) is very effective for social anxiety disorder. CBT focuses on how thoughts, feelings, and behaviors are linked, and teaches you tools to manage all three. You will learn more about some of these tools in Chapters 3, 4, and 5. ERP is a special type of CBT that helps you approach activities you have been avoiding in a gradual and manageable way. You will learn more about ERP in Chapter 6.

You are the expert on you; no one knows you better. An important part of CBT is that it aims to make you not only the expert on you but also the expert on your own treatment. In this book, you will learn how and why these skills work. There will be activities throughout the book to help you practice what you learn.

You also may want to consider meeting with a mental health clinician, such as a psychologist who specializes in CBT with ERP to help you use the tools. Although this book does not replace treatment with a psychologist, it can still help you find your inner fierce. Keep in mind that some of the tools in this book may feel more useful than others, and one tool will not be a fit for every situation. The goal is to fill your mental toolkit with many different skills so that you have options.

FOCUS ON YOUR VALUES

Before we launch into setting goals about what changes you would like to see after reading this book, it can be helpful to reflect on what you value first. Values are experiences or ways of being that you consider important. By identifying what is important to you, you can create goals to help you do more of what you value.

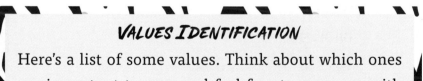

VALUES IDENTIFICATION

Here's a list of some values. Think about which ones are important to you, and feel free to come up with others—this isn't an exhaustive or complete list. There are no right or wrong values, and everyone will have a different list, just as people have different favorite colors, foods, movies, and books. You deserve to do what is meaningful to you.

ACCEPTANCE	FRIENDLINESS
ADVENTURE	GENEROSITY
APPRECIATION	GROWTH
ASSERTIVENESS	HEALTH
AUTHENTICITY	HONESTY
COLLABORATION	INDEPENDENCE
CONNECTION	KINDNESS
CONTRIBUTION	LEARNING
COURAGE	MASTERY
CREATIVITY	OPEN-MINDEDNESS
CURIOSITY	PATIENCE
DETERMINATION	PERSISTENCE
ENJOYMENT	RESPECT
EQUALITY	ROMANCE
FAIRNESS	SELF-CARE
FLEXIBILITY	SKILLFULNESS
FITNESS	SPIRITUALITY
FORGIVENESS	TRUST

SET GOALS

Now that you have identified some values, you can create goals for yourself to help you do more of what is important to you. Set yourself up for success by developing "SMART" goals. These goals are:

Specific
Measurable
Achievable
Relevant
Time-Bound

If you selected the value "learning" and have difficulty participating in class, you might say, "My goal is that I would like to participate in class more." Remember to make the goal as specific and measurable as possible. How often is "more?" If you have not been participating in class at all, think of how often it would be reasonable to participate after working on some skills for several weeks. Setting a goal to participate once in every class every weekday may seem like a big leap, so think of a more manageable goal instead. For example, perhaps you might start off with a goal of raising your hand one time in your favorite class five days per week and aim to achieve this goal in the next three months. That goal is specific (raising your hand in your favorite class), measurable (one time each weekday), achievable (participating in a favorite class may be less intimidating than other classes), relevant (participating in class is consistent with the value "learning"), and time-bound (you'll achieve this within three months from now).

Reminding yourself of your values and goals is not only useful in developing a plan to tackle social anxiety, it can also be helpful for staying motivated. If you find yourself on tough days asking, "What's the point?," review your values and goals to reenergize yourself. For some extra practice, see if you can help Jordan develop a goal based on his value in the "Putting it Into Practice" box. Keep an eye out for additional "Putting it Into Practice" boxes in future chapters for more opportunities to test out skills learned.

PUTTING IT INTO PRACTICE

"That used to be me. I really miss playing soccer. I want to start playing again, but I don't feel ready."

What could be a **SMART** goal for Jordan as a starting place to get back into playing soccer? On the next page is one example:

S(pecific): Play soccer with my best friend at the park for 30 minutes three days a week.

M(easurable): Play for 30 minutes after school three days a week.

A(chievable): I can ease my way into playing with just one person around.

R(elevant): I will get to play soccer during the week for fun without the additional performance pressure.

T(ime-Bound): I will try this for the next month before I take my goal to the next level (like play with a larger group of friends or play with the same friend more often each week).

DEVELOP "SMART" GOALS CONSISTENT WITH YOUR VALUES

Pick three of your values, and try to come up with a value-driven "SMART" goal for each one. Keep these goals in mind as you read this book to help with motivation. After you have reached your goals, you can revise them and develop new "SMART" goals that help you take the next step forward, such as by doing your desired activity for more days in the week, for a longer period of time each day, with more people, etc. If you find you have difficulty reaching a goal, revisit the goal and see if it needs to be tweaked to be more specific, achievable, etc. It's okay to start small—in fact, it's great, because you're more likely to set yourself up for success!

IN A NUTSHELL

There are tools to help you take charge of your life and do what's important to you. The first step is to make a plan.

* Identify what values are important to you.
* Set goals that are Specific, Measurable, Achievable, Relevant, and Time-Bound.
* Start small (achievable) and work your way up to bigger goals.

Next, we'll look at why we even have emotions and how they affect the body.

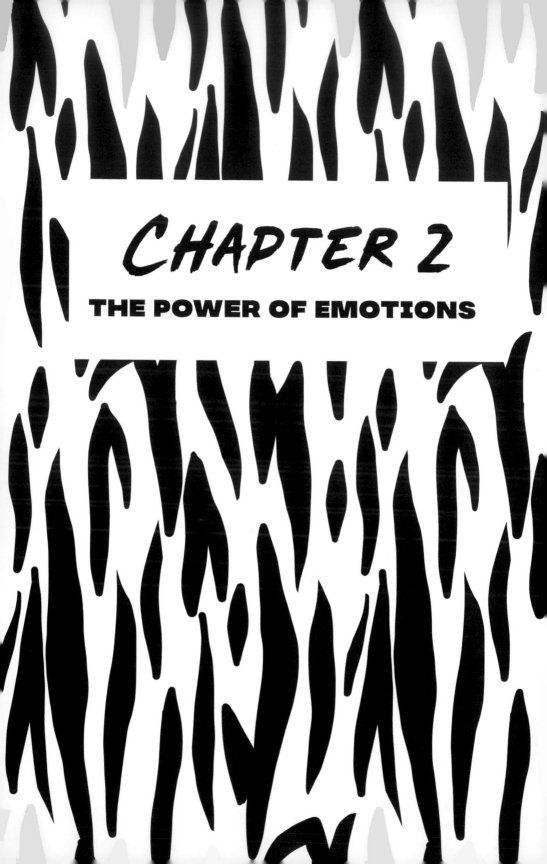

CHAPTER 2

THE POWER OF EMOTIONS

You may wish to get rid of anxiety altogether, but we actually need anxiety in smaller doses. Before you start working on how to keep your anxiety in check, it can be helpful to know what purpose anxiety serves in the first place—and for that matter, what roles your other emotions play in your life. Researchers have argued that there are seven universal emotions that people from all over the world experience and express, and each one serves a purpose. You need emotions to communicate not only with yourself but also with others.

IDENTIFYING EMOTIONS

Let's take a look at each of the seven emotions, and for each one, think about how you express it and why it might be useful for you.

HAPPINESS

Happiness allows us to experience joy and connect with others around shared experiences. Expressing happiness invites company and also communicates that we like what is happening.

SADNESS

Sadness makes us vulnerable. When we are vulnerable, we open ourselves up to bonding with others. If you just talked about the weather all the time with people, you wouldn't be able to get to know them well or feel close to them. Sharing your experiences, including sadness, can allow you to feel closer to someone else and get the support you need to cope with a challenging time. For example, if you let someone know that your best friend moved away and you're feeling sad and lonely, they might support you and keep you company.

FEAR

You might think that this emotion is wrecking things for you, but it's important in moderation. Fear keeps you safe when there are threats. Think about when you need to cross the street—a small dose of fear is what helps you remember to look both ways.

You also might be wondering what the difference between fear and anxiety is. Both fall under the same emotion umbrella and alert the body to react, but different situations call upon each one. Fear shows up when you're faced with a safety threat right then and there, like when there is fire in a building. Anxiety includes worries about something possibly happening in the future, such as worrying that people will think you're stupid when you participate in class. Anxiety actually can be useful in moderation, too. When you have a test the next day, some anxiety can help motivate you to study.

ANGER

Many people think this emotion only creates more problems. When anger is expressed ineffectively, such as by yelling and name-calling, that can be true. Anger can be useful, though, when expressed effectively, such as by communicating what you need respectfully. Anger allows you to protect yourself by setting boundaries that keep people from walking all over you. For example, it might make you angry when a friend uses one of your belongings without asking. Anger could push you to tell them that you'd rather they ask first next time, and that communication can help you protect what is important to you.

DISGUST

This emotion also keeps you safe. When you open up a carton of milk that has spoiled, it is helpful for you to find the smell disgusting and not drink the spoiled milk. Yuck!

SURPRISE

Surprise can be either welcome or unwelcome. You might be pleasantly surprised when someone throws you a surprise birthday party, and you might be surprised in an unwelcome way when a friend, who usually sits with you at lunch, decides to sit with someone else. This emotion allows you to communicate with others how an experience felt and decide where to go from there. For example, your excited and surprised expression at the party might show your friend that you appreciated their efforts. Your sad and surprised expression at lunch might lead your friend to talk with you after lunch and iron out a friendship wrinkle.

CONTEMPT

This emotion conveys that you do not approve of someone else's behavior. Contempt can be necessary when standing up for what's important to you. For example, you might disapprove of a bully who picks on your friend. By standing up for your friend, you show that the unkind behavior will not be tolerated. You know what deserves some contempt? Your anxiety, when it tries to bully you. This book will teach you some skills to stand your ground and have that bully of anxiety back off!

Lots of people find it difficult to figure out what emotions they are feeling in the moment, so some practice identifying emotions can be helpful.

PUTTING IT INTO PRACTICE:

Identify which emotions Jordan, Emma, and Maria are feeling in the situations below:

Emotion key: *happiness, anger, surprise, sadness, disgust, fear, and contempt.*

THE MIND AND BODY CONNECTION

Emotions can serve as tools to communicate with others, and they can also be used to send signals to your body to make sure it reacts the way you need it to. But sometimes, the signals misfire and don't go the way we want. Right before heading into a social situation, such as going to a birthday party, giving a presentation in front of your class, or ordering at a restaurant, have you ever been worried and then noticed your body reacting in a way, like sweating, that makes you feel even more stressed about possible embarrassment? It is very common for people with social anxiety to worry about how their body will respond when they feel anxious around others.

It turns out there's an adaptive, or helpful, reason why your body reacts this way when you're afraid. Let's rewind back to prehistoric times. When an early human would face danger, such as a tiger in the jungle, an alarm bell in the brain (in the sympathetic nervous system) would set off the fight-or-flight system. The early human would then flee (the "flight" option), and the body rallied to help the person escape as quickly as possible. Their heart may start racing to pump blood to the arms and legs and help them run away. The person might feel dizzy, as blood flows away from the brain and instead to the arms and legs. The person may sweat, which helps them keep cool and also makes them slippery and more challenging for the tiger to catch. Even feeling the need to throw up or have diarrhea could be helpful: they make a person as light as possible, so they have less weight to carry when trying to escape quickly.

Fast-forward to now, and our brains still have that alarm system. Thankfully, we usually don't meet any tigers, but we need that alarm system in place when there are other threats to our safety. For example, we need the alarm bell to go off when there is a fire so that we get ourselves to a safer place.

Sometimes, though, the signal misfires, and it's just a false alarm. With social anxiety, the brain sounds its alarm to tell you that there's a threat to your safety when, in reality, there's no threat. Your body may start sweating before that presentation or birthday party because the alarm bell is sounding, just as if you were about to have to outrun a tiger. This book will help you look for evidence to figure out when there's a real threat versus when your body is sending a false alarm.

PANIC ATTACKS

Sometimes, feared social situations, such as giving a presentation or going to a party, can set off a panic attack. A panic attack is when you experience a rush of at least four of the symptoms listed below, usually peaking within minutes:

* Faster heart rate and/or a pounding heart
* Sweatiness
* Shakiness
* Shortness of breath
* Choking sensations
* Nausea or other stomach distress
* Hot or cold flashes (e.g. chills)
* Numbness or tingling
* Feeling like things are not real or not attached to your body
* Fear of dying
* Fear of losing control
* Fear of having a heart attack

The body sounds the alarm because it thinks there is a threat to its safety, and that sets off a panic attack. There are ways to teach the brain when the alarm isn't needed—you'll learn these techniques in future chapters.

IDENTIFY ANXIETY IN THE BODY

It can be helpful to practice identifying where in your body anxiety shows up in social situations. You can use those symptoms as signals to check whether it's just a false alarm. Scan your body from head to toe, and think about how it reacts when you feel anxious. Maybe your face gets hot, your hands become sweaty, and you feel butterflies in your stomach. What are some common places anxiety shows up in your body? Is it these or other places? If you haven't paid much attention to the specific sensations before, try it out. You can draw how your body feels when you're anxious on your own sheet of paper to practice having this awareness and to help you make the most of tools discussed in future chapters.

IN A NUTSHELL

Learning the power of emotions and their connection with the body is a great first step to forming a foundation that you can use as a platform for skill building.

* There are seven basic emotions that everyone feels.

* Your emotions can cause physical changes in your body

* Sometimes our minds send out false alarms, and we feel anxiety or panic.

The next chapter will teach you how thoughts are also connected to feelings and behaviors and show you some new skills.

CHAPTER 3

KEEPING THOUGHTS IN CHECK

_F_eelings and behaviors are connected to each other, and thoughts are connected to both of them, too. This chapter will teach you how thoughts, feelings, and behaviors are linked, ways to identify your own thoughts, and tools to change unhelpful ones.

THREE-COMPONENT MODEL

The three-component model below is the foundation of CBT, which teaches you tools to help you manage your thoughts, feelings, and behaviors and do what's important to you. In the diagram below, thoughts, feelings, and behaviors are connected by double-sided arrows to show that each one can influence the other.

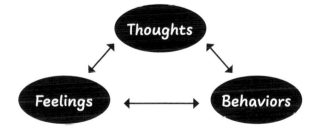

Let's use an example to bring this model to life. Imagine Maria, the 13-year-old you met earlier in the book, is walking down the school hallway and her best friend, Sophie, bumps into her shoulder, says nothing, and keeps walking.

What is one thought Maria could have? Maybe she thinks, "Sophie must be mad at me." How might Maria feel if she had that thought? She might feel worried, sad, and angry about the situation. What would Maria's behavior look like at lunch? Maybe Maria would avoid Sophie and sit elsewhere. What do you think Sophie would think about Maria then? Sophie now might think Maria is mad at her and avoid Maria. Just one thought in one moment could feed a vicious cycle.

Let's rewind and take a look at that situation in a different way. After Sophie bumps into Maria, does not say anything, and keeps walking, what is another thought Maria could have? Maria might think, "Maybe she was in a rush to class" or "Maybe she didn't see me." How might Maria feel now? Maria might be in a neutral state, and at lunch, she might sit with Sophie and see how her day has been so far.

Was the action in the first situation any different than the second situation? Did Sophie bump into Maria harder or say something mean? No. The situation didn't change; the way Maria perceived or thought about the situation changed. Of course, it could be possible that Sophie *is* mad at Maria; but the key is to think about how *helpful* it is to have that thought when you don't know all the facts. How helpful is it for Maria to stew over that thought while she's in math class and can't know whether Sophie is mad or was just late to class? Part of CBT will help you learn to look for evidence that supports your thoughts, and another part will help you select more helpful thoughts so that your feelings are kept in check.

CONNECTING THOUGHTS TO FEELINGS

It takes some time to learn how certain thoughts can make you feel (one part of the three-component model). It may seem obvious, but sometimes we react without actually stopping to identify our feelings, which can get in the way of what we really want. Practicing this skill can help you catch yourself before having unhelpful experiences. Try matching some example thoughts to corresponding feelings below to work on building this new skill muscle.

Thought	Feeling
I have a major project due tomorrow, and I'm not done with it yet!	Happiness
He should be ashamed of himself.	Sadness
My best friend is switching to a different school.	Fear
Whoa, that came out of nowhere!	Anger
My team just won the national championship!	Disgust
She just cut in front of me in line!	Surprise
This strawberry is moldy.	Contempt

Key: Fear, Contempt, Sadness, Surprise, Happiness, Anger, Disgust

TRACKING THOUGHTS, FEELINGS, AND BEHAVIORS

Now that you've practiced connecting example thoughts and feelings, the next step is to identify all three linked thoughts, feelings, and behaviors. Being able to recognize how all three are connected will help you work on changing them, a skill that you'll learn later in this chapter.

Thoughts usually pop into your mind quickly and feel automatic, so it's often tough to catch your thoughts when you have them. You might find it easier to start with noticing when your emotions or behaviors change. Are you aware when your heart races, your face gets hot, and you sweat, but you're not sure why? These changes can signal you to stop and wonder what you might be thinking.

Let's go back to Maria's example to explore how this could work. Maybe Maria notices she's feeling worried, sad, and angry. Once she becomes aware of that, she reflects and realizes that she thought Sophie was mad at her. When she thinks that, she then observes that she avoided Sophie at lunch. What Maria's doing here is practicing a thought record, a way to track your thoughts as well as connected feelings and behaviors, to help prepare you for making changes in the future.

Below is an example of what a thought record might look like for Maria. It's like a horizontal version of the three-component model. The first column is a description of the situation. The second column is where you write what emotions you are experiencing and how intensely you are feeling them (on a scale of 0–10, with 10 being the most intensely you could experience the feeling). The third column is for the thought, and the fourth column is where you record the behavior.

SITUATION	FEELING(S) (0–10)	THOUGHT	BEHAVIOR
Best friend bumped into my shoulder and did not say anything	Worried (9), sad (5), and angry (6)	She must be mad at me.	Avoided my best friend at lunch

THOUGHT RECORD

Create a record like this one on a separate page. Complete the blank rows for a couple recent times when you noticed you were feeling any emotion. It might be useful to practice completing some rows in a thought record at the end of each day to rehearse this skill.

UNHELPFUL THOUGHTS

We have been talking about how thoughts are connected to feelings and behaviors, and sometimes those thoughts can be unhelpful influences on your mood and actions. Brains are presented with so much information all day long that they need to take shortcuts by focusing on certain parts to avoid experiencing information overload. If you walk into a classroom, you probably look for an empty seat and sit down in a chair. It would be a lot for you to walk in, take in how many ceiling tiles there are, count how many light bulbs are lit, notice what everyone is wearing, focus on the noises you hear, etc. Instead, your brain takes shortcuts by narrowing its focus on just what it thinks it needs in the moment. Sometimes, those shortcuts go awry when the brain makes conclusions based on what it sees while also missing key information. This can wreak havoc on our emotions.

Let's go back to Maria in the hallway. Her brain took a shortcut and concluded that Sophie must be mad at her just based on Sophie bumping into Maria's shoulder without saying anything. Sophie might be mad at Maria, but does Maria have any information that proves that would be true? Maria's brain just assumed that might be the case because it was one possibility, but based on the little information Maria has, there could be lots of other possible reasons, like Sophie being late to class. In this case, Maria's brain's shortcut led to Maria assuming the worst.

Soon we'll talk about how, like Maria, you can also change some of your thoughts to help you feel better. But before we do that, let's look at some common unhelpful thoughts that people have. This list exists for a reason; many people have these thoughts! You are not alone if any seem familiar.

BLACK-AND-WHITE THINKING: Thinking that something is either "all good" or "all bad" with no gray areas in the middle.

> **Example:** If I don't make a basket every time I shoot a basketball, then I'll never make any team!

SHOULDS AND MUSTS: Beating yourself up about what was or was not done.

> **Example:** I shouldn't have said that.

FOCUSING ON THE NEGATIVE: Missing the positive in a situation.

> **Example:** The whole day was terrible because I forgot what I was going to say when the teacher called on me in class.

CATASTROPHIZING: Jumping to negative conclusions, assuming that the worst-case scenario will happen, and/or reacting to a situation as if it were the end of the world.

Example: If I forget a line in my presentation, I will fail the class. If I fail the class, I will never graduate from high school and will be jobless for the rest of my life!

OVERGENERALIZING: Assuming the outcome of one experience will be the same for all experiences.

Example: She broke up with me; everyone I date will dump me.

EMOTIONAL REASONING: Making a conclusion based on a feeling.

Example: I feel embarrassed, so I must have done something wrong.

LABELING: Defining yourself based on an outcome or a quality of an event.

Example: My friend did not ask me to do anything this weekend; I am a loser.

MIND READING: Assuming you know what others are thinking.

Example: He looked at me when I asked that question. He thinks I'm stupid.

PERSONALIZATION: Blaming yourself or someone else for a situation that is not entirely within any one person's control.

Example: We lost the soccer game because I didn't play my best.

Which unhelpful thoughts stood out to you as ones you tend to have? Which one do you think Maria had?

Let's check out the chart below to see which unhelpful thought may have come up for Maria.

SITUATION	FEELING(S) (0–10)	THOUGHT	UNHELPFUL THOUGHT NAME
My best friend bumped into my shoulder and did not say anything	Worried (9), sad (5), and angry (6)	She must be mad at me.	Mind Reading

Sophie never said that she was mad at Maria; instead, Maria assumed she knew what was going on inside of Sophie's head. Maria's unhelpful thought type was mind reading.

PUTTING IT INTO PRACTICE

Which unhelpful thoughts do you notice Jordan having? Keep an eye out for two different ones.

If you said, "catastrophizing" and "mind reading," then you spotted them. Jordan was catastrophizing by assuming the worst-case scenario for his piano recital. He also was mind reading by assuming that he knew that his teacher would be disappointed in him.

I can't go to that piano recital. I am going to mess up, and everyone will be looking at me while I do it. I will make a total fool of myself, disappoint my teacher, and will never be allowed to show my face and perform there again!

STOP, DROP, AND ROLL

You have been practicing noticing what you are feeling and thinking; now you'll learn how to change unhelpful thoughts into more helpful ones. Your thoughts can try to boss around your feelings and behaviors. In order to push back, you'll need to act like a scientist looking for data. What kind of data? When you have a thought, think about whether you have all the information you need to support that thought. Your job is to find out whether the thought is true and/or helpful. How do you make that happen? We'll use a phrase that you probably learned to help you practice fire safety: "Stop, drop, and roll."

STOP.

When you notice your emotions changing, *STOP*. Reflect on what you might be thinking. See if your thought was an unhelpful thought from the list above. If it was an unhelpful thought, channel your inner scientist, and ask questions to find out if there were any data to support the thought or if it was helpful to you.

Here are some possible questions you can ask for each type of unhelpful thought:

Black-and-White Thinking

Are there other possible perspectives?

Are there any options in between the two extremes?

Shoulds and Musts

Does beating myself up about this change the situation?

Is this just a rule I make for myself and that doesn't apply to everyone?

Focusing on the Negative

Did I miss any positive things?

Am I being too harsh or critical?

Catastrophizing

Am I 100% sure that the outcome will happen?

Are there other possible outcomes?

What evidence do I have that this will happen?

Overgeneralizing

Does one experience mean that every experience will be the same?

Have there been other times in my life when this did not happen?

Emotional Reasoning

What facts do I have to support this?

Has a feeling of mine ever misguided a thought before?

Labeling

Does one event define me?

Are there other experiences I have had that would not support this label?

Mind Reading

What proof do I have that person has that thought?

Can I read minds?

Personalization

How do I know that this is about me?

What evidence do I have that I am responsible for this outcome?

DROP.

If there were limited data and/or the thought was unhelpful, *DROP* it. If it wasn't helpful, it doesn't deserve your focus.

ROLL.

Once you've dropped an unhelpful thought, *ROLL* with a more helpful thought. You can come up with more helpful thoughts by using answers to the questions you asked of the original thought.

Emotion changes→ **STOP**→ *"What am I thinking?"*→ *"Which unhelpful thought is that?"*→ *Question the thought* → **DROP**→*"What is a more helpful thought I could have?"*→ **ROLL**

Let's go back to Maria's situation to put this skill into practice. After Sophie bumps into Maria's shoulder, does not say anything, and keeps walking, Maria may notice that she starts to feel worried, sad, and angry. Once she becomes aware of her mood changing, she will **STOP** and ask, "What am I thinking?" Once she realizes that she thinks Sophie is mad at her, Maria checks what unhelpful thought that might be. We learned earlier that it was mind reading. Now that Maria knows she was trying to read Sophie's mind, she can ask herself, "What proof do I have that Sophie is mad at me?" or "Can I read Sophie's mind?" Maria could answer, "I don't have any proof that Sophie is mad at me, and I definitely can't read Sophie's mind." She might then ask, "Are there other possible reasons she bumped into me and didn't stop?" There are; Sophie could be late or may not have even seen Maria. Once she realizes this, Maria can **DROP** the unhelpful thought and **ROLL** with the more helpful thought she got from the last question: "Maybe she was late to class."

After you "Stop, drop, and roll" with a more helpful thought, re-rate how intense each of your previously identified feelings are, and see if the ratings are any lower than when you started. Let's put this into practice using Maria's experience.

SITUATION	FEELING(S) (0–10)	THOUGHT	UNHELPFUL THOUGHT NAME	ALTERNATIVE THOUGHT	NEW FEELING(S) (0–10)
Best friend bumped into my shoulder and did not say anything	Worried (9), sad (5), and angry (6)	She must be mad at me.	Mind Reading	Maybe she was late to class.	Worried (2), sad (1), and angry (0)

In this example, Maria felt less worried, sad, and angry when she thought Sophie might be late to class. The situation did not change; how Maria thought about the situation did. Shifting how you think about a situation can give you some power to change your mood. Sometimes an original thought is not true, and you can drop it more easily once you realize you don't have data to support it. Other times, the thought may be true, but it still isn't helpful to stew on it. If you can distance yourself from an unhelpful thought even just a bit, the intensity of your emotions may lower. Your anxious feelings may not drop all the way to zero, especially when you don't know the real answer yet, but they can come down a few notches and make a situation more manageable.

For example, let's say Sophie said, "I *am* mad at you." Maria now has data to support the original thought. Maria could soak in this thought, feel very anxious, and think about every past action to try and figure out what she might have done to make Sophie mad at her. If Maria did that, she probably would not pay attention in her next class, would feel more worried, sad, and angry because she was focusing on how Sophie was mad at her, and still wouldn't know for sure what the answer was.

How could Maria *DROP* the "She's mad at me" thought and *ROLL* with a different thought? Maria could think, "I'm not sure what I did to make Sophie mad at me. Wondering what I did without a chance to ask her won't help me focus on math class. After class, I'll ask Sophie why she's mad at me and apologize if I need to." Maria probably won't be skipping off happily to math class when she has this thought, but she might feel a little less worried, sad, and angry than when she started because she's shifting her focus back to class. After math, she plans to return to this topic when she has an opportunity to gather more information. The situation still did not change; the way Maria thought about the situation changed.

PUTTING IT INTO PRACTICE

Let's return to Jordan's catastrophizing and mind-reading thoughts about his piano recital. Help Jordan drop his unhelpful thoughts by rolling with more helpful thoughts. Below are some ideas:

Catastrophizing: "I am going to mess up, and everyone will be looking at me while I do it. I will make a total fool of myself... and will never be allowed to show my face and perform there again!"

More helpful thoughts: "No one plays piano pieces spot-on every time, and all I can do is try my best. I don't know of anyone who has been kicked out after making a mistake. I might feel embarrassed if I make a mistake, and I can make sure to practice more after the recital to try to improve for next time."

Mind reading: "I will disappoint my teacher!"

More helpful thoughts: "My teacher has never told me that she's disappointed in me when I make mistakes. If she doesn't say it, I don't have proof that she feels that way. Plus, teachers are there to help you learn from mistakes. If I were supposed to know everything already, why would I be taking lessons from her? I can show my teacher how much I care and want to do my best by asking her for extra help when needed."

In a Nutshell

Now that you've learned how thoughts, feelings, and behaviors are connected:

* Use a thought record to keep track of your thinking patterns.

* Identify unhelpful thoughts.

* Practice *STOP*, *DROP*, and *ROLL* to move forward with more helpful thoughts.

It can be helpful to practice "Stop, Drop, and Roll," nightly using examples that happened earlier in the day to get the skill muscle in shape for when you need to use it during a future emotion-filled moment—something that can be tough to do when the skill is new. The next chapter also will teach you skills that you can use in any present moment.

CHAPTER 4

MINDFULNESS

S ocial anxiety can be suffocating with all of the self-criticisms and worries about others making judgments. Mindfulness can help you turn your mind away from those judgments and back to the present moment.

What is mindfulness? Mindfulness is purposefully and nonjudgmentally paying attention to the present moment (rather than the past or future). Practicing mindfulness trains the brain to focus and use its attention in a helpful way by noticing without judging. Judging your surroundings would be labeling something as "good," "bad," "right," or "wrong." When you notice something mindfully, it's not good or bad; it just is.

THE PURPOSE OF MINDFULNESS

The goal of mindfulness is not to relax. Relaxing is one possible outcome, but that is not the aim of the skill. Mindfulness enhances your awareness and attention in a way that helps you learn from an experience and not make it needlessly worse. Anxiety often causes you to worry about the future, and as you learned in the previous chapter, getting stuck with unhelpful thoughts typically doesn't help your mood. Focusing on unhelpful thoughts just increases their power. Using mindfulness, or paying attention to the present moment without judging yourself, can keep those thoughts from becoming too overwhelming.

HOW TO USE MINDFULNESS

To see how mindfulness can be helpful, try this experiment. Think about anything you want for the next 15 seconds. You can think about anything in the world except for a pink polar bear. Ready? Start thinking about anything other than a pink polar bear!

How did it go? I suspect that pink polar bear popped up in your thoughts. Have you ever heard someone say, "Just don't think about it"? If it were that easy, you would have done that ages ago! Unfortunately, telling yourself not to think about something tends to backfire. When you tell your mind not to think about something, it wants to think about it

Telling yourself not to think about worries will just make your unhelpful thoughts show up more often. Instead of telling you not to think about it, mindfulness brings your attention back to the present moment without judgment.

What's so special about this present moment? Imagine being stuck in traffic and worrying that your teacher will be mad that you're late to class. If you focused all your attention on being late to school and your teacher's reaction, a thought about the future, would the cars move any faster? No. Would you feel more miserable? Yes. What could you do instead? Describe what you see in the present moment using all five senses: sight, touch, hearing, smell, and taste. Notice the colors and shapes of the vehicles around you (sight). Feel the texture of the seat (touch). Listen to any noises you might hear, such as the humming of a vehicle's engine (hearing). Smell any scents inside the vehicle, such as aromas from any of the foods you packed for lunch (smell). Describe the flavor inside of your mouth, perhaps something that is lingering from breakfast (taste). If you focus on what is going on around you in the present moment, you are not making yourself feel worse by focusing on unhelpful, distressing, and future-oriented thoughts unnecessarily.

Mindfulness takes practice. As humans, our minds wander naturally. There's a good chance that while trying to notice the present moment in that car, your mind may wander back to "I'm going to be late." That's OK. Part of mindfulness is working on noticing when your mind wanders away from the present moment and gently (rather than judgmentally) bringing your attention back to the present moment. If you have the thought, "I should not be thinking about the past or future; I should be thinking about the present," that is a judgment in the "Shoulds and Musts" category of unhelpful thoughts. A gentle approach would be to simply notice, "My mind just wandered to thinking about the future. I am going to bring it back and look at what's around me." Each time you notice your mind wandering and gently bring your attention back to the present moment, you help strengthen that focus muscle.

MINDFULNESS EXERCISES

Below is a list of different mindfulness exercises you can try, and there are countless more. If you are paying attention to the present moment on purpose and non-judgmentally, then you are doing mindfulness! You can practice mindfulness skills anytime—especially when you find yourself dreading social situations, like going to a party, class, or extracurricular activity. For any of the following exercises, if you notice your mind wandering, gently bring your mind back to the present moment.

MINDFUL EATING

Have you ever watched a movie while eating a bag of popcorn and then felt surprised once your hand reached the bottom and no more was left? We often eat while focusing on something else—sometimes unhelpful thoughts about the past or future. Eating mindfully using all your senses can keep your focus on the present moment. Because you eat regularly, food can also be a helpful reminder to practice your mindfulness skills.

Find a piece of wrapped candy (you can also use a small piece of food, such as a chocolate chip, marshmallow, or raisin) for this exercise. Imagine you are an alien from another planet and have never seen this item until now. Using all your senses, starting with sight, describe what you see. Notice the colors and shapes on the wrapper. Next, rub your fingers on the surface of the wrapped candy and notice whether it's smooth or rough. When you press the candy between two fingers, notice whether it's hard or soft. Next, bring the wrapped candy to your ear and rub it between two fingers. Notice the sounds, such as crinkling, you hear. Unwrap the candy, and bring it to your nose to use your sense of smell. Describe the scent. Remember to describe the candy nonjudgmentally, with phrases like "It smells fruity," rather than "It smells good" or "It smells bad." Next, place the piece of candy on your tongue and close your mouth. Don't chew it or move it around yet! Notice how the candy tastes. Notice how it feels on your tongue. You might experience the candy melting and changing shape. If it's a chewy piece of candy, bite down slowly and notice the change in sound and texture as you munch. See how long you can make it last and how long you can keep noticing new sensations.

You just made one piece of candy last quite a while! Have you ever spent that long eating one piece of candy before? My guess would be no. By using this skill, you keep your focus on the piece of candy and away from what might happen in the future or what already happened in the past. Try eating mindfully with any other food, and see what your experience is like.

PUTTING IT INTO PRACTICE

"Those girls are looking over at me; they're probably talking about how I'm such a slob for the way I'm eating these pretzels. I am a mess. There are crumbs everywhere, ugh!"

How can Emma keep her focus on the present moment instead of on these worries? See if you can help her try to eat those pretzels mindfully. Below is one example.

Emma could think to herself, "The pretzel is hard. It feels smooth in some places and bumpy in others where there are salt crystals. The pretzel has round edges and three openings in the center. It's also twisted toward the top. The pretzel has a toasted smell, and I hear crunch sounds when I bite down on it. The pretzel tastes salty and has a rough texture during the first few bites. I notice my saliva forming around the pretzel bits in my mouth, and it makes the pretzel softer as I chew."

Where was Emma's focus during the mindful eating exercise? Her focus was on the pretzels—not on wondering what others were thinking of her.

5, 4, 3, 2, 1

You can practice the 5, 4, 3, 2, 1 exercise anywhere, without anyone knowing it. Wherever you are, find five things of the color of your choice, such as red. Perhaps you spot a red chair, book, pen, backpack, and shirt. Next, identify four things that are another color, such as blue. Maybe you see a blue water bottle, marker, rug, and pair of pants. Then, find three things of another color, such as green. Continue doing this exercise until you have found two things of another color and then one item of a final color. This is another way to keep your focus on the present moment.

MINDFUL DAILY ROUTINES

Sometimes, we go through the motions of our routine activities without focusing on them. Perhaps you ride your bike the same route to school each day. You've taken that route so many times that the rehearsed routine frees up space for your mind to think about something else until you get to school. That something else might be a worry about all the tests you have that day and that you'll let your teachers down if you don't do well. Those thoughts are "What if" situations and create extra distress that you don't need. What deserves to be front and center on your brain's stage is the present moment: the texture of your bike's handlebars, the smell of the fresh air, the sounds of birds chirping, the taste of syrup on your lip left over from the pancakes you had for breakfast, and the colors of the houses you pass on your route to school. Practicing mindfulness during everyday routines will help you pay attention to the journey and not the endpoint.

Many people wonder how they'll find time to practice new skills like mindfulness. You don't need to add anything to your schedule to try this one; you can practice shifting your focus during activities you already do! You can use mindfulness during any daily routine, such as showering or brushing your teeth. While you are showering, pay attention to the smell of the shampoo, and focus on how it feels to massage the shampoo through your hair. Notice the lather that may form as you massage your scalp. Observe the shape and color of the shampoo's lather running down your body as you rinse it out of your hair. Focus on the temperature and pressure of the water as it touches your scalp.

When you're getting dressed for school, if you have the thought, "People will think I have no style if I wear this shirt," use mindfulness to return your focus to the present moment by noticing how soft and stretchy that red shirt you just put on is. Mindfulness is there for you when you find your mind racing through all potential stressful experiences you might have at school that day while you're in the shower, brushing your teeth, or getting dressed. Practicing mindfulness during any of those routine activities can help keep you grounded in the present moment.

RESISTING THE URGE

Has someone ever told you to resist the urge to scratch a bug bite because scratching it would make it worse? You may have found trying to keep your fingers off the itchy bite to be very uncomfortable, especially at first. Perhaps resisting became more manageable over time because you learned you could do it and that the bug bite would go away eventually. This urge-resisting mindfulness skill can apply to your anxiety, too. Anxiety often creates an urge to avoid situations that make you uncomfortable. You might have the urge to leave a class, party, or restaurant because you're worried about being embarrassed, but if you keep leaving class, your brain will think that you can't handle staying. Plus, you might fall behind in school and feel even worse, just like how that bug bite will get worse if you keep scratching it.

What if you went urge surfing, or focused on the urge until the wave of its intensity rode itself to shore? All waves must come down, and your urges and anxiety do the same. It might feel like a big wave at first, but over time, you would learn that you could handle something like staying in class. By focusing on and riding out that urge, you teach your brain that you can do it. This may sound like a big task, but we'll talk about how to break down surfing urges into approachable steps by starting with smaller waves first in Chapter 6, when we discuss ERP. For now, you can practice resisting urges in ways that may not create as much anxiety.

Try practicing this skill by using a piece of sour candy. Place the sour candy on your tongue, and then keep your mouth closed for two minutes while resisting the urge to spit out the candy. Use your senses to stay focused on the candy, and notice any urges you might have. See if you can surf the urge and focus on how the candy tastes and feels in your mouth. If any judgments pop up, such as "I am terrible at this," gently bring your mind back to the present moment and nonjudgmental position, such as "This candy makes my face pucker."

What happened? You might have discovered that the candy became less sour and turned sweeter over time. Think about how that might relate to your anxiety. Perhaps it is very uncomfortable to stay in class when you have the urge to leave, but after you spend more time in class, you learn that you can handle sitting there, you get to see your best friend in the class, and you stay on track with your schoolwork.

MINDFULNESS EXERCISE PLANNING

It can be helpful to start with one mindfulness exercise to practice at the same time of day each day. For example, you could practice mindfulness every time you shampoo your hair in the morning or use mindful eating during breakfast. Pick which skill you want to practice and when you'll use it. You can make a chart like the one below to help yourself keep track.

MINDFULNESS SKILL	TIME OF DAY
Mindful hair shampooing	7:00 a.m. while in the shower
5, 4, 3, 2, 1	7:30 a.m. during my walk to school

IN A NUTSHELL

Mindfulness is a skill to help you settle your mind, and you can use it anytime without anyone noticing. Practicing mindfulness each day when you're relatively calm can help you strengthen the skill muscle. That way, it will be in shape to use when you notice yourself starting to have suffocating thoughts and want to shift your focus away from them.

* Mindfulness can come in many forms, like mindful eating, paying attention more during daily routines, and urge surfing.

* You can plan a mindfulness schedule to help get into a habit of using mindfulness.

* Find a mindfulness practice that works for you, and remember not to judge yourself.

The next chapter will teach you skills that will help settle your body.

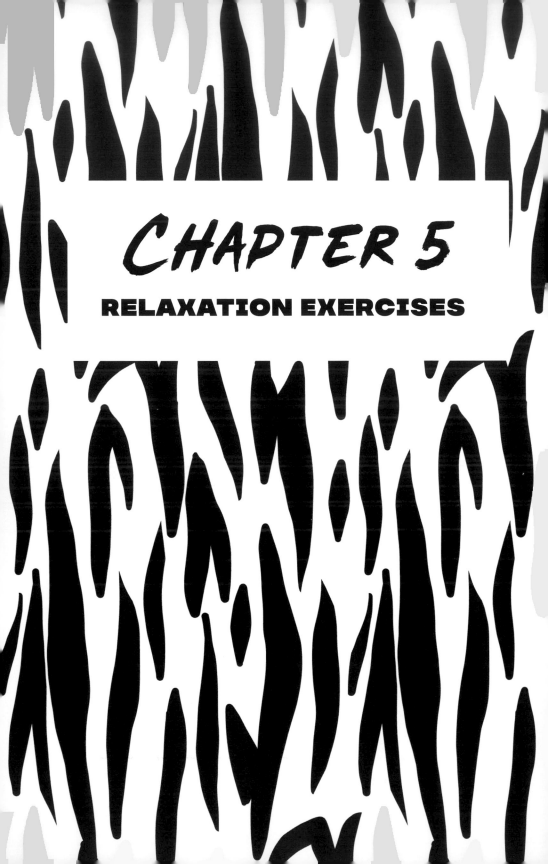

CHAPTER 5

RELAXATION EXERCISES

*R*elaxation exercises are tools to help you bring your stress levels down a few notches. They can be especially useful when you're worrying about an upcoming social activity later in the day or trying to fall asleep while worries just won't let you be.

NO, DON'T "JUST BREATHE"

Has someone ever told you to "just breathe," to help you relax, and when you tried to breathe like usual, you didn't feel better? If so, you're not alone at all. When people are feeling anxious, it's very common for them to take breaths of air from their upper chest, which can make them feel even worse. You may be able to get away with that type of shallow breathing while feeling calm, but breathing repeatedly that way when you're stressed may make you have shortness of breath or even hyperventilate. That can be extra stressful. Below are some techniques that might help make "just breathe" actually useful.

Some might feel dizzy when first learning to practice multiple rounds of a new breathing skill. If you feel dizzy, pause the skill, stay seated, and breathe like you usually do. When the dizziness subsides, you can try the skill again. After you've practiced the skill a bit more, you may find that the dizziness is less likely to happen.

DIAPHRAGMATIC BREATHING

This type of breathing can send a signal to your brain to turn on a calming system called the parasympathetic nervous system. Before we go over how to do diaphragmatic breathing, first check out how you typically breathe. Place one hand on your upper chest and one hand on your belly. Inhale deeply through your nose and watch which hand rises higher than the other. If your hand on your upper chest moved higher, you took a shallow breath from there. Remember, this is common, especially when one is feeling anxious, so you would not be alone at all if this happened for you. To maximize your breathing or get the most air in your lungs, you need to use your diaphragm, which is a muscle beneath your lungs that helps them expand and breathe more deeply. When you do this, the hand on your belly will move higher when you inhale.

You can practice this by lying down and placing a box of tissues or a thin book on top of your belly. Imagine there is a balloon in your belly and that you want to inflate that balloon as much as possible with a single breath. Inhale deeply through your nose and see if the box of tissues on top of your belly goes higher. If it did, you inflated the balloon. Once you have inflated the balloon, deflate the balloon as slowly as possible by exhaling through your mouth. Have you ever let go of an inflated balloon? If so, you may have watched it fly all over the room until it deflated fully. That balloon was out of control. You want to practice breathing with control. Try exhaling as slowly as possible, as if you only opened your two fingers pinched at the end of the balloon a tiny bit. You can try making the sound of the letter "S" or a hiss to let out only a little bit of air at a time to practice this skill at first, until you get better at controlling the amount of air you exhale.

Practice inhaling deeply through your nose and exhaling slowly through your mouth. Try to make the exhale last longer than the inhale—that sends a signal to the brain to turn on the calming-down system (parasympathetic nervous system). Notice your belly inflating and deflating, and observe the ways your body may be settling.

Box Breathing

Another type of breathing relaxation exercise involves "drawing a box" with your breath while using diaphragmatic breathing. You first select a number of seconds, such as three. Next, you inhale through your nose for three seconds, hold your breath for three seconds, exhale through your mouth for three seconds, and hold your breath again for three seconds. It's a "box" if you think of the inhale as going up, the holds as staying flat (or going across), the exhale as going down, and the next hold as staying flat (or going across in the opposite direction as the other hold). You can repeat this exercise a few times in a row. You can start with three seconds for each step and increase each step to four seconds after some practice. Once you get used to doing each step for four seconds, you may choose to increase the number of seconds to five or six, but keeping the number at four seconds works, too. It's about finding the number that works best for you.

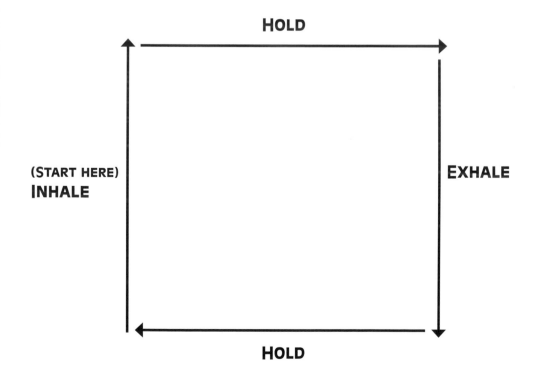

PUTTING IT INTO PRACTICE

"Oh, no, I just made eye contact with James... JAMES! Of all people, I accidentally had to look over at the cutest guy in my grade?! Face, meet palm. Now he must know I like him and is thinking that I'm pathetic because I'm a nobody. Am I blushing? I must be blushing. Oh, no, that's going to make it worse. I've really done it now. Where's a hole to crawl into when you need one?!"

Maria's unhelpful thoughts and body's stress response are off to the races! Maria can rein them in and slow down their pace by drawing boxes with her breath.

"Breathe in through my nose for four seconds, hold my breath for four seconds, exhale through my mouth slowly for four seconds, and hold my breath for four seconds. Rinse and repeat."

PROGRESSIVE MUSCLE RELAXATION

When you feel anxious, it's common for the body to feel tense. Catching your body when it starts to feel tight can be a cue that stress levels are ramping up and that it might be helpful to bring them down a few notches. In progressive muscle relaxation (PMR), you loosen up muscle tension by starting with relaxing one part of the body and then slowly adding in other parts of the body. The idea is that by having your body physically relaxed, the mind will follow suit because the two are so connected.

When using PMR, you first tense one part of your body on purpose. For example, you clench your hands into fists as tightly as you can and hold the fists for 10 seconds. Next, you unclench the fists and notice the release in tension. It might seem a bit backward to tense your muscles up if you were already feeling tense, but by tightening the muscles as much as possible, you are gathering all of the tension into a bundle so that you can let it all go together. You may feel looser than when you started. You can also think of progressive muscle relaxation as progressive muscle tension-release.

If you are sitting in a chair, have your feet flat on the ground. When you start to clench one part of the body, practice inhaling using your diaphragmatic breathing. When you clench, inhale; when you release the clench, exhale. Your breath will be in sync with your tension.

Here's a step-by-step procedure for how to practice PMR; usually you work your way in order through the whole body. You might find it helpful to read through the whole thing before you try it, so you can get an idea of the overall pattern of PMR.

1. To start, curl your toes underneath your feet and try to get them as close to the soles of your feet as possible while you inhale. Hold that position for five seconds by counting slowly (one, one thousand, two, one thousand, three, one thousand, etc.). Next, uncurl your toes and notice the tension release as you exhale. Release the tension all at once, not gradually, so you can really notice the difference in feeling.

2. Move to your calves. Press your toes into the ground and raise your heels so that your calves move upward. Notice the tension gathering in your calves while you inhale and hold the tension for five seconds. Next, bring your heels back down to the ground and exhale.

3. For your thighs, lift your feet off the ground, as if to make room for an imaginary footstool, and tense your thighs while you inhale. After five seconds, release the tension and lower your legs while you exhale.

4. Next, squeeze your bottom as tightly as you can for five seconds and then release the tension.

5. To clench your stomach, try to pull your muscles inward as if someone were stepping on your stomach. After holding the tension for five seconds, release the muscles.

6. With your hands, imagine you are squeezing every last bit of lemon juice out of some lemons by clenching your fists tightly for five seconds. Release the hold on the lemons and unfold your fingers.

7. For your upper arms, imagine you are lifting a dumbbell weight to do a bicep curl. Close your fists, and with your palms facing upward, pull your fists toward your shoulders. Hold the tension for five seconds and then release the hold on the reins.

8. Now, arch your back as if someone were running a feather from the bottom to the top of your back to tickle you. Hold your arched back for five seconds, then bring your back to its resting position.

9. Next, raise your shoulders all the way to your ears to tense your shoulders and neck muscles for five seconds until you lower your shoulders as far down to the ground as you can let them go.

10. Finally, scrunch your face muscles as if you just ate the sourest lemon in the world. Press your eyelids down, crinkle your nose, and pucker your lips. Hold the tension for five seconds until you release the muscles.

11. After you have tensed each muscle group individually for five seconds, start with your toes again, and add on each muscle group one at a time until you're tensing everything at the same time as you inhale one big breath. Hold all of the tensed muscle groups together at the same time for five seconds, and then exhale and shake your body out as if you were one giant wet noodle. Notice the release of tension in your body.

WHEN TO USE RELAXATION EXERCISES

It takes a lot of practice to be able to use relaxation exercises when you need them. Just like with the thinking tools, it can be helpful to rehearse the skills when you are feeling fairly calm so you can use them properly when you need them in the future.

Once you have the skills sharpened and ready in your toolbox, you can use them to help you wind down before bed or before you're in a situation that you fear. You might want to practice the skills an hour before a soccer game, play performance, birthday party, or date.

Relaxing the body before you head into a stressful situation, such as a soccer game, will allow your body to have more resources to approach it. If your brain fires a false alarm and signals the body to prepare for a safety threat several hours before the game, your body will spend a lot of energy trying to deal with it, which will make it extra difficult to play the way you want during the game. Relaxation skills can help settle the body so you can use that energy to do activities you want to do, such as scoring that soccer goal.

It's best to use relaxation skills well before a feared activity starts. Using relaxation skills when you're right in the middle of a feared situation will distract you from a key learning opportunity that will show you that you've got what it takes to keep approaching the activity.

RELAXATION EXERCISE PRACTICE

Now that you've learned about some relaxation skills, you can practice them. Pick a time of day when you might feel relatively calm and will have time to practice a skill. Choose how long you want to practice. Describe how your body feels before and after you use the skill, and rate how intensely your body feels that way on a scale from 0 (not at all) to 10 (the most intensely you have felt that way). Notice if your body feels any different afterward. Here's an example chart; you can make a similar one on a piece of paper to keep track of your skill rehearsal.

TIME OF DAY	RELAXATION EXERCISE	DURATION OF SKILL	HOW MY BODY FEELS BEFOREHAND (INTENSITY RATING)	HOW MY BODY FEELS AFTERWARD (INTENSITY RATING)
8:00 p.m.	Diaphragmatic breathing	Five minutes	Tension in my chest (8)	Tension in my chest (4)
9:00 p.m.	Progressive muscle relaxation	Two minutes	Tension in my limbs (7)	Tension in my limbs (3)

In a Nutshell

Relaxation skills can help you slow your thoughts and emotions, and make you feel more prepared to face what worries you.

* Breathe using your diaphragm in order to make the most of each breath and activate the parasympathetic nervous system.

* Progressive muscle relaxation is another way to signal the body to relax.

* Practice calming tools well before or after the feared activity, not during.

The next chapter will teach you more about what is helpful to do *during* those feared situations to ensure you have key learning experiences.

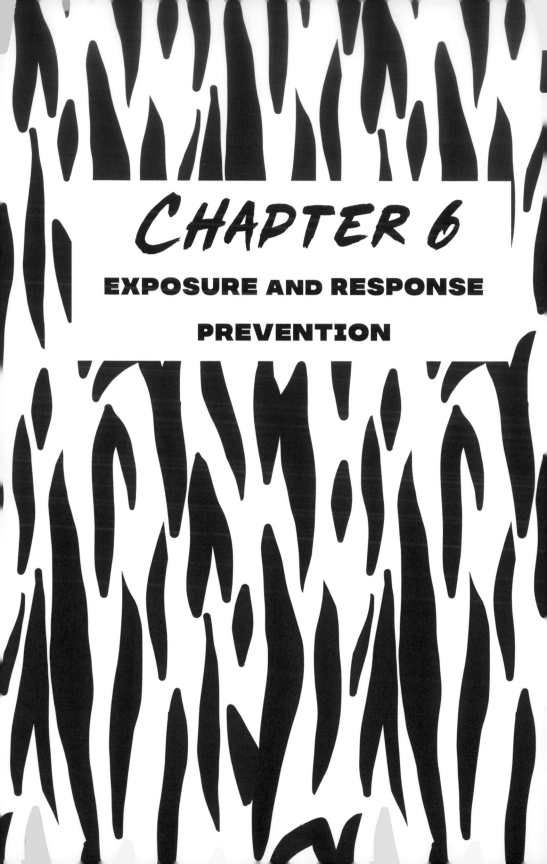

CHAPTER 6

EXPOSURE AND RESPONSE PREVENTION

*S*o far you have been learning mindfulness and relaxation skills that you can use before or after stressful experiences. This chapter will teach you how to approach stressful experiences so that you can be in charge of your life and do more of what you value.

Exposure and response prevention (ERP) is a gradual process that goes at your pace. ERP encourages you to approach your feared situations one step at a time; these steps are called "exposures." It also helps stop you from responding in a way that might make your anxiety stronger, such as by avoiding a situation. ERP might sound terrifying at first, but it may seem more doable once you learn how it works. ERP is designed to go at a pace that you decide, so exposures will feel more approachable.

Imagine you're at a swimming pool, and it's a bit chilly out. If I asked you to jump in the deep end, you might think, "No way!" because it would feel like a big shock. What if instead, I asked you to dip your big toe in the shallow end? How would that feel at first? If you thought that your toe might feel cold at first, but then would get used to the temperature of the water after several minutes, you'd be right. What would happen if you dipped your next toe in the water? You'd have the same experience of adjusting to the temperature of the water. Imagine yourself easing into the swimming pool up to your knees, up to your waist, and then up to your neck. At this point, if I asked you to dunk your head, you might be more willing to do so. Why? You got used to the temperature of the water, so the deep end now seems more approachable. Your whole body got wet by easing into the swimming pool, just as it would have if you had jumped into the deep end. Jumping into the deep end, however, would have been a shock to your system. ERP is like starting with your big toe in the shallow end by doing an approachable exposure and easing into the swimming pool with more exposures at your pace.

SUBJECTIVE UNITS OF DISTRESS SCALE

A way to measure how challenging each exposure is for you is what is called SUDS. They aren't soap suds—SUDS stands for "Subjective Units of Distress Scale." It's a scale that measures distress, with "units" ranging from 0–10, with 10 being the most distressed one could feel. It is subjective because it is how you feel, and no one knows that better than you!

You can think of SUDS as a feelings thermometer. We'll use this temperature rating scale to gauge which situations are more or less distressing for you. For example, imagine what your SUDS might be if you were watching your favorite TV show at home while eating your favorite food. Your SUDS might be around zero, right? Now imagine yourself singing the National Anthem at a packed baseball stadium. I suspect your SUDS would be higher than zero for that one.

INHIBITORY LEARNING MODEL

ERP is based on the inhibitory learning model, which suggests that an exposure works by the brain learning that the exposure either was not as bad as expected and/or that you could handle the exposure.

Imagine that your brain has highways made from experiences, and the neurons (the nerve cells that talk to other parts of the body) in your brain are the cars. When you approach school, for example, and turn right back around to avoid it, a highway forms that tells the brain that school is dangerous. The more that you avoid school, the more you pave the avoidance highway, and neurons drive on that highway more often.

When you do an exposure, it's as if the brain puts up a "Do not enter" sign at the avoidance highway. The brain starts paving a new highway, the approach highway, as you learn that going to school wasn't as bad as you expected—or at least was doable. Every time you have that learning experience, more cement gets paved on the approach highway. The neurons also learn to drive on that highway more often.

Remember that the avoidance highway won't disappear in the brain. Sometimes on windy or stressful days, the "Do not enter" sign gets knocked down, and the neurons start driving on the avoidance highway again (avoiding instead of going to school in this example). All is not lost. With some skill rehearsal and exposure practice, you can put that "Do not enter" sign back up, remind the brain that school is not as bad as expected and that you can handle going there, and redirect your neurons back to the approach highway instead.

A key point to remember about the inhibitory learning model is that it emphasizes that your SUDS don't need to lower for the exposure to work. In fact, your SUDS could have been higher than you had expected, and the exposure still could have been successful. The key piece is for your brain to learn that you were able to do the exposure. Even though your anxiety may try to convince you that you won't be able to, bringing out your fierce and doing the exposure anyway will prove the anxiety wrong. A completed exposure is a successful exposure, no matter what your SUDS are at the end. If you learned that the outcome either was not as bad as you expected, or that it was doable, then you nailed it!

OVERLEARNING

Before we start brainstorming exposures, let's talk about a concept called *overlearning*. Overlearning teaches your brain that even in situations that are above and beyond everyday experiences, the brain can handle them. It's an important part of an exposure plan.

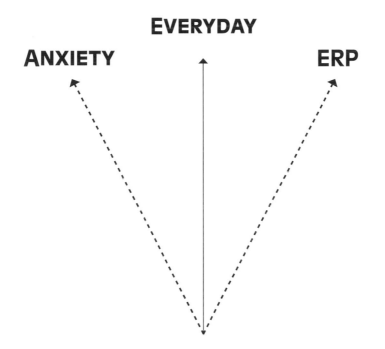

EVERYDAY

ANXIETY   **ERP**

Do you know anyone who has made a New Year's resolution? You can probably think of more than one person. Do you know anyone who has kept the resolution for an entire year? You might not be able to think of anyone. That's because humans tend to drift from plans. Let's say someone's New Year's resolution is to go to the gym every day. After January 1st, they are strong out of the gate and go to the gym every day for a week. One day the following week, they are really tired and decide that they'll skip the gym but will go the next day. In time, they go three days a week, then two days a week, and then one day a week. Eventually, their gym routine consists of sitting on a couch, reaching for a potato chip, and bringing the chip to their mouth. Imagine the biceps after those arm curls!

If you practiced only everyday behaviors while doing exposures, there would be room for you to drift toward what anxiety pulls you to do, like avoid situations. That would mean you would move from the straight arrow (everyday) of the diagram on the previous page to the arrow to the left (anxiety). Instead, we want to do exposures that are above and beyond the everyday, or the arrow to the right (ERP), to give you room to come back to the everyday when you drift.

If Jordan, the 15-year-old, who stopped participating in class because he worries about giving the wrong answer, only practiced the everyday exposures that involved raising his hand when he was sure of the answer, he might drift backward and be right back to not raising his hand in class at all. What should he do? He should do some overlearning exposures. Jordan would gradually work his way up to raising his hand and giving the wrong answer on purpose. You might think that sounds ridiculous, but stay with me here! The everyday aim is to give a correct answer, but this exposure would teach Jordan's brain that even in the extreme case—getting an answer wrong—he could handle it. Practicing overlearning exposures leaves room for Jordan to drift backward a little bit and still be ahead of where he used to be.

The brain needs overlearning exposures to learn that it can handle a wide range of experiences. Overlearning exposures will help keep the anxiety in check when it tries to take control. That is why we will plan not only exposures to help you with the everyday, but also exposures that are above and beyond the everyday to help give you room to drift.

FEAR-FACING LADDER

All this talk about facing fears may make you wonder how you would go about doing it. We'll break this down into steps, just like how you would ease into a swimming pool. Below is an example of a fear-facing ladder for Emma, the 16-year-old with a fear of asking people questions. It's important to note that even people with the same fears won't have identical fear-facing ladders; they vary, depending on which situations are challenging for each person. Here's an example; start at the bottom rung of the ladder, or a SUDS of 1, and read upward until you reach the top of the ladder, or a SUDS of 10, to see how these exposures build on each other.

SUDS	BEHAVIOR
10	Asking a stranger where the local pharmacy is while standing in front of it
9	Calling a 24-hour pharmacy and asking what time it closes
8	Raising my hand in class and asking the teacher to explain one of the words or concepts used
7	Asking a classmate how her weekend was
6	Stopping a stranger on the sidewalk and asking for the time
5	Asking a grocery store employee where the loaves of bread are
4	Calling a restaurant and asking what time it closes
3	Asking my same-aged cousin what his favorite movie is
2	Asking my uncle what his favorite food is
1	Asking my grandmother how her day was

You'll notice toward the top of the ladder there are examples of overlearning exposures. Asking an employee at a 24-hour pharmacy what time it closes (when the pharmacy is always open) is not an everyday behavior; it is an extreme action to teach the brain that it can handle potentially embarrassing situations. Unfortunately, not everyone in this world will respond kindly to every question, so it is key to create some exposures to prepare you. The exposures will help you practice getting possibly unkind or snarky responses and showing yourself that you can do it even when you feel uncomfortable.

It's understandable to worry about people judging you while you do these exposures, and you might think, "That person will think I'm weird for the rest of her life" after you ask her when the 24-hour pharmacy closes. After the exposure, you can bring out your inner fierce and talk back to your thoughts. There are two responses to your thoughts that can be useful if you have this worry. Please note that these are responses to your *thoughts* and *not* to the person in the pharmacy: you want to take the high road, or kind route, when talking to others. Anxiety does not deserve your kindness, though, so bring out your fierce side and put that anxiety in its place!

- *"That person should get a hobby."* If that store employee spends all her time thinking about you asking that question, then you might feel sorry for that employee. People don't typically spend every moment of their lives thinking about a question someone else asked. Even though you may feel embarrassed and focused on the question, that store employee is likely focused on her own life. People usually focus on themselves.

- **"That person has room for growth."** If someone spends time being unkind to someone else, then that person has room for growth or improvement. Knowing that may not take away the sting you feel after getting an unkind response, but keep in mind that person's behavior likely reflects something about that person and not about you. People who are unkind to others typically do not feel good about themselves. They may try to make others feel worse than they do as a way to make themselves feel better.

PUTTING IT INTO PRACTICE

"How in the world am I going to be able to try out for the travel team next month? That's like launching myself to the top of Mount Everest!"

Jordan can prepare for trying out for the travel team by creating a soccer-based fear-facing ladder—try making one as if you were him. Remember to include some overlearning exposures at the top of the ladder to help Jordan learn that he can handle situations above and beyond what he would usually experience. The top of the mountain or ladder will seem closer and more within reach with every next step that Jordan takes.

   Here's a list of exposure ideas. Feel free to use any of these and/or come up with some exposure ideas of your own to add to Jordan's ladder.

- Play soccer with my best friend at a park when no one else is at the park.
- Try my best during a pick-up soccer game with friends.
- Play soccer in my backyard by myself.
- Purposefully kick the soccer ball to the left of the goal instead of into the goal while playing with a friend.
- Play soccer with my best friend at the park when the park is crowded.
- Purposefully kick the soccer ball to the left of the goal during a pick-up game with friends.

CREATING A FEAR-FACING LADDER

Try creating a fear-facing ladder for your own social anxiety by making a blank ladder on a separate piece of paper. You can have multiple behaviors on the same rung (SUDS level). For example, you might find that ordering a meal at a restaurant and eating a yogurt in the school cafeteria each would be a SUDS level of 6, or that raising your hand and giving the wrong answer on purpose (an example of overlearning) and giving a speech in front of the class both are a SUDS level of 10.

If some exposures feel too challenging to approach, try to find ways to break them down into digestible steps. If asking a peer, "How was your weekend?" in the school hallway feels too tough, start with making eye contact and smiling. The next step might be making eye contact, smiling, and waving "Hi." After you have tried those two steps, maybe asking that student how their weekend was will feel more approachable because you took a few steps up the ladder first and didn't jump right to a high step.

Check out these examples of exposures for Emma (who avoids ordering in restaurants, raising her hand in class, and eating in the cafeteria) that are broken down into steps to give you ideas:

Goal: Eating in the cafeteria during lunch

Drink a beverage→ eat a yogurt→ eat a peanut butter and jelly sandwich→ eat one crunchy pretzel at a time→ eat two crunchy pretzels at a time→ eat even crunchier carrots→ eat a flaky pastry that might leave crumbs→ eat a turkey sandwich that has extra meat inside that could fall out→ eat a sloppy joe→ eat a sloppy joe while purposefully leaving some sauce on your cheek (overlearning).

Goal: Answering a question in class

Raise your hand in your favorite/most approachable class when you are 100% sure of the answer→ raise your hand in your favorite class when you mostly are sure of the answer→ raise your hand in your favorite class when you are unsure of the answer→ raise your hand in your favorite class and purposefully give the incorrect answer (overlearning)→ repeat this list of exposures for your next-favorite class→ repeat this list of exposures for each class.

Goal: Ordering in a restaurant

Order a pre-set meal at a drive-through restaurant→ order a pre-set meal at a fast-food restaurant's counter service→ order a meal as described on the menu at a sit-down restaurant→ order a meal off a menu at a sit-down restaurant and ask to substitute one ingredient for another→ order a meal off a menu at a sit-down restaurant and then change your mind to a different meal→ order a meal off a menu at a sit-down restaurant and ask to substitute one ingredient for another when the menu says, "No substitutions" (overlearning).

SAFETY BEHAVIORS

During an exposure, it's important to focus on what you're doing so your brain can learn that it's not as bad as you expected and that you can handle it. Sometimes, instead of focusing this way, people use safety behaviors to lower their anxiety, but these can actually keep exposures from working. Safety behaviors don't let you learn that you can do the exposure on your own. For example, say I think I can only go to school if I have my lucky penny (my safety behavior). When I get to the front door of school and realize that I left my lucky penny at home, what will I think? "There's no way I can go to school without my lucky penny!" Is it my lucky penny that's helping me go to school? No, but my brain thinks it is because my brain has not learned that I can go to school without it.

Returning to the swimming pool analogy, think of safety behaviors as wetsuits. Wetsuits help keep surfers and scuba divers warm. If you wore a wetsuit while easing into the swimming pool on a chilly day, your body would not be exposed to the temperature of the water and would not learn that it could swim in the pool without the wetsuit.

Other examples of safety behaviors might be avoiding eye contact while talking to people, having a friend or family member with you when you talk to others, or counting backward from 100 while attending a school dance. All of these behaviors distract the brain from the exposure and prevent the brain from learning that the behaviors or people aren't necessary. The relaxation techniques you learned earlier can also be safety behaviors, which is why it's important to do them well before or after the exposure, not during.

Avoiding or running away from an experience can be a very common safety behavior. It makes sense, as approaching can feel terrifying. Avoiding may seem like it protects us, but it unfortunately actually makes the problem worse. Imagine yourself standing in the water at a beach, and a big wave starts approaching you. Your instinct may be to run to shore. What ends up happening? That big wave is faster and can pull you underwater. What should you do? It may seem like it goes against all instincts, but you should face the wave and dive into the sweet spot. That way, the wave can glide over you and allow you to get to the other side. That's what is needed for facing anxiety. Instead of running to shore, face anxiety head on, without using safety behaviors. The only way out is through.

PUTTING IT INTO PRACTICE

What's Maria's safety behavior in this situation? If you said, "Looking down at her feet" or "Avoiding eye contact," then you would be right!

What could Maria do instead to learn that the hallway is not a danger zone? She could look straight ahead and notice all the colors and shapes that she sees, an example of mindfulness.

IN A NUTSHELL

ERP can help you channel your inner fierce and start doing more of what's important to you. By creating opportunities to learn that social situations are not as challenging as expected or at least are doable, your brain will realize that it had been firing false alarms and that with practice, you can approach class, parties, the mall, sports, and more!

* Exposures are measured using SUDS.

* You can create an exposure plan by making a fear-facing ladder with challenges of increasing SUDS levels.

* Overlearning is a key part of an exposure plan and helps keep you from sliding back to where you started.

* Remember not to use safety behaviors during exposures!

You'll learn how to do an exposure and make the most of it in the next chapter so that you can do more of what you value.

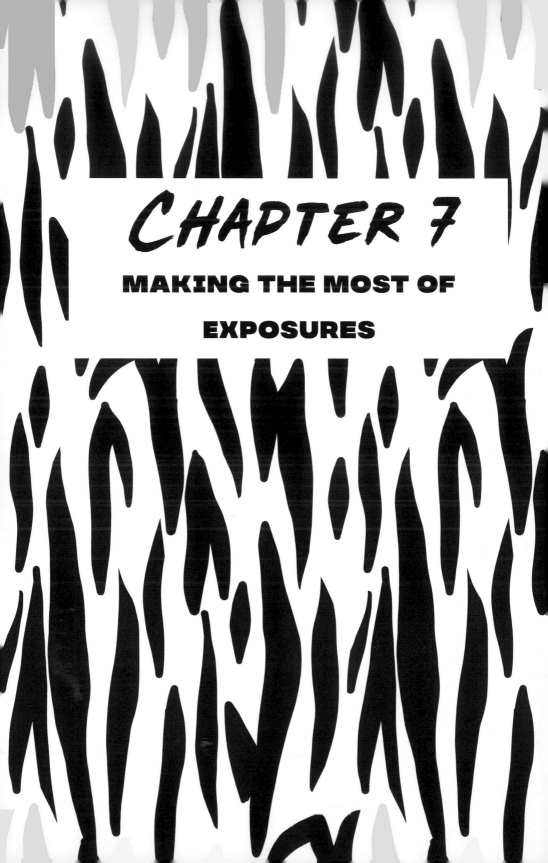

CHAPTER 7

MAKING THE MOST OF EXPOSURES

*N*ow that you've learned what an exposure is and how ERP works, this chapter will show you how to do an exposure. We'll talk about how to make the most of learning opportunities—the key to paving more cement on the approach highway in the brain— for each exposure. You'll also learn how to keep fueling your motivation to approach your fears.

HOW TO DO AN EXPOSURE

There are steps to take before, during, and after an exposure, and we will go through each. Before we get to the steps, pick an exposure you'd be willing to start with, and keep in mind that choosing a behavior that's a SUDS level of zero for you won't be very useful. You want to expose yourself to *some* anxiety to create a learning experience. Instead, you can start with a slightly higher, yet still approachable SUDS level, such as a SUDS level of four, to get your feet wet in the swimming pool.

Before you do an exposure, ask yourself or write down what you're worried will happen and what you expect your SUDS to be.

During an exposure, it's important to practice mindful awareness of the present moment. It may be tempting to distract yourself from the discomfort, but remember, that's a safety behavior. Pay attention to your surroundings and how your body feels in the moment. Practice noticing without judging, such as, "I notice that I am making eye contact," versus the judgment, "This is terrible!" Your mind may want to jump to what it's worried will happen in the future—if it does, bring your focus back to the present moment, the exposure.

After an exposure, congratulate yourself. You did it! Next, rate your SUDS after the exposure and compare the rating to what you predicted your SUDS would be before the exposure. You might see that your SUDS were lower than expected if the exposure was not as bad as you anticipated. But even if your SUDS were higher than you expected, a completed exposure is a successful exposure. Way to go!

After the exposure, revisit the worries you had before the exposure. This is important for the learning process, or the highway-building in your brain. Ask yourself if what you were worried about actually happened. For example, if you worried that someone would yell at you for asking for the time, you would be embarrassed forever, and you would not be able to handle it, check and see if those things happened. Anxiety usually overestimates the likelihood of something bad happening. If your feared reaction did happen, such as someone giving you a dirty look or laughing at your question, ask yourself whether you learned that you could handle the experience even if it made you feel uncomfortable. If you did, it was a successful exposure. The processing after the exposure teaches your brain that the situation is doable.

PUTTING IT INTO PRACTICE

"That was humiliating! I was so awkward up there during my audition. I totally bombed that exposure. Why did I even bother? This is just another example of why I should never audition for plays in the first place."

Emma is feeling demoralized after doing an exposure of auditioning for a play. Was the exposure a bust because she felt uncomfortable? See if you can come up with some statements Emma can use to boss back her anxiety. Below are some ideas, too:

"Feeling awkward doesn't make it a failure."

"I did the exposure, so that actually makes it a successful one."

"I learned I could do it even though it was uncomfortable."

"I am out of practice, and more practice will help me get back into my performing groove."

TRACKING YOUR EXPOSURES

Sometimes, it can be helpful to have a visual of how your SUDS change over time after you do an exposure several times. You can use a graph like the one below. The x-axis, or horizontal line, is each exposure trial, such as asking a stranger for the time. Before you start, you mark on the y-axis, the vertical line, what you expect your SUDS to be, such as 6. The first time you do the exposure, you rate what your SUDS were afterward. For example, say your SUDS were a 5. Mark where the 1 of exposure trials and 5 for SUDS intersect. If the second time your SUDS were a 4, mark where the 2 of exposure trials intersects with the 4 for SUDS. You can continue charting your SUDS each time you do an exposure to see if you can observe any patterns. Sometimes, like in this example chart, your SUDS may

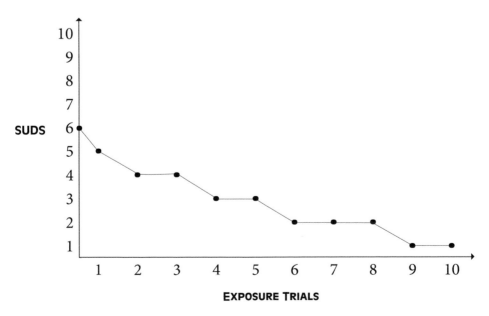

decrease over time. Remember that the exposure is still successful even if your SUDS increase over time, because your brain has learned that you can do it.

GET THE BIGGEST BANG FOR YOUR (EXPOSURE) BUCK

Here are some tips for maximizing the learning experience from an exposure:

1. **Use mindfulness.** Paying attention to the present moment without judgment will help your focus remain on the exposure so you learn that you can do the behavior. Practicing mindfulness also can help keep your mind from wandering to the future, where anxiety can live. During an exposure is when you can practice urge surfing. Focusing on the present moment and the exposure will allow you to realize that you've got this and help you ride that wave to shore.

2. **Do not use safety behaviors.** Avoiding the use of safety behaviors will help your brain learn that you, and not something or someone else, crushed that exposure. You deserve the credit!

3. **Eventually pair exposures together.** Combining exposures can create a bigger impact. Once you have done exposures separately, you can pair them together. For example, say you're afraid of walking down a school hallway when other students are there and of asking a peer a question. After you do each of those exposures separately, try walking

down a school hallway while asking a peer what she did over the weekend.

4. **Plan overlearning.** Creating exposures that are above and beyond everyday behaviors will teach your brain that even in extreme scenarios, you can do it.

5. **Change your environment.** Practicing an exposure in a variety of settings will help your brain learn that you can do the exposure anywhere, not just in one particular place. For example, say you are worried about ordering at a restaurant. If you just practice ordering at the same restaurant, your brain may think you can only order there. Instead, practice ordering at many different restaurants and different kinds of restaurants (fast-casual restaurants, sit-down restaurants, etc.).

6. **Label your emotions.** Identifying how you're feeling during an exposure can help you experience lower levels of emotions. Labeling how you're feeling, such as, "I'm feeling worried" or "I'm feeling embarrassed," not only keeps the brain mindfully focused on the present moment, but it also rallies support from a part of the brain that does some thinking (the executive functioning corticol areas) so that it can manage the emotion part of the brain (the limbic system). By identifying how you're feeling in the moment, it's as if the thinking part of the brain tells the emotion part to "simmer down!"

PUTTING IT INTO PRACTICE

"Sophie just picked my worst nightmare for her birthday party— dinner at a restaurant and then a movie at the mall!"

How can Maria make the most of exposures to prepare her for her friend's birthday party? What are some steps she could take? Below are some ideas that use the six ways to get the most out of exposures—feel free to come up with other ones, too.

1. Eat mindfully at restaurants.

2. Make eye contact with and then smile at each person who walks by the dinner table.

3. Eat popcorn at the food court in the mall. On another day, go see a movie at the mall. Next, eat popcorn while in a movie theater.

4. Purposefully trip, stumble, spill some popcorn, and catch yourself while looking for your seat in the movie theater.

5. Eat dinner at a variety of popular neighborhood restaurants on different days and at different times.

6. Identify how you're feeling while passing by people you know in the mall (for example, "I am feeling worried.")

REWARDS

We've been talking about how to approach stressful and tough experiences. It can be helpful to have a reward system in place to motivate you to try challenging exposures. Whether you are 9 minutes or 99 years old, you're never too old to be rewarded for effort. Even adults need rewards—they certainly don't go to work for free! And a lot of stores reward customers with punch cards or points to get them to keep coming back. Rewards work for people of all ages and encourage you to keep doing certain behaviors.

Think about some motivators that make you more likely to continue working on exposures. For example, if you really love ice cream, but find it difficult to order at a restaurant, you could plan an exposure that encourages you to order at an ice cream store. After ordering, you get to eat one of your favorite desserts; the exposure has a built-in reward.

To set up a reward system, brainstorm a list of rewards and decide how much each is worth. Each exposure will earn you one "star," and each reward should be worth a different number of stars. The rewards don't necessarily have to cost money; they can be things like picking what you want for dinner or having a day without chores. Your parents may have to participate if you do those kinds of rewards, of course; they can assign how many stars or points each reward is worth. Because desired rewards can often require a parent's permission, having a parent involved may allow you to work toward something really motivating. You can earn a star per exposure, or a parent can decide whether the more challenging exposures closer to the top of the ladder might be worth more than one star. You don't necessarily need a parent involved, though, if your rewards are something you can decide to do or get for yourself.

It can be helpful to cash in your stars a couple times per week to keep yourself motivated. If you find that you want to save your stars for a larger-ticket item, you can have a system that double-counts the smaller-ticket items: the stars used for rewards that don't necessarily cost money can be used again for the rewards that are worth more stars and cost money. For example, the five stars used to pick what you want for dinner at home can be used toward the 50 stars it takes to go out to dinner at your favorite restaurant. The idea is to have a system that encourages you to use your stars multiple times per week so you remain motivated.

REACH FOR THE STARS

Whether you use a structured reward system or not, it can be helpful to have a visual way to keep track of exposures you've planned and rewards you'll earn. Below is an example of a chart that Emma started for recording her upcoming exposures. For your chart, you can write the exposure in the left column and then add stars, tallies, checks, or any mark you want in the boxes under the days of the week when you do the exposures.

	MONDAY	TUESDAY	WEDNESDAY	THURSDAY	FRIDAY	SATURDAY	SUNDAY
Raise hand in class	★						
Order in a restaurant							
Eat lunch in the cafeteria							

You can also make a chart to list some reward ideas that will help motivate you to approach exposures. It can be helpful just to see the things you're working towards written down.

5 STARS	10 STARS	15 STARS	20 STARS	25 STARS	50 STARS	100 STARS
Choosing dinner	Having dessert before dinner	Picking the movie for family movie night	Having a day of no chores	Going out for ice cream	Going out to dinner at my favorite restaurant	Getting a one-month subscription to a music-streaming service

PREPARING FOR ANXIETY'S DEFENSE

There will be a time when you get into your exposure groove and feel like an exposure rock star. You may think, "I'm killing it!" The next day, you may wake up and feel extra anxious, all the way back to where you started, and demoralized. That's because anxiety is like a bully, and bullies do not like to be threatened. If a bully were used to getting lunch money from Jordan, and one day Jordan decided to stop giving the bully lunch money, the bully would probably not say, "OK, that sounds good" and walk away. Instead, the bully would put up an even bigger fight. Similarly, when you nail those exposures, anxiety will try to fight back with a vengeance. You might feel worse before you feel better. It may seem like you're back to the start, but you're not. You have more tools and learning experiences than when you started. This is the time to keep doing exposures and moving forward so that you can show your anxiety that it's not the boss of you. Bring out your fierce side, and put that anxiety in its place!

IN A NUTSHELL

Exposures help you manage your anxiety so you can be the boss of you. Remember:

* Challenge yourself with exposures that cause your anxiety some discomfort but are still approachable.

* Keep track of your exposures to show your progress.

* Set up a reward system to keep yourself motivated. Your hard work deserves it!

But keep in mind that the approach highways you're paving can be bumpy when anxiety doesn't feel like it's in charge. In the next chapter, we'll talk about how to prepare for anxiety's defense so that you can keep moving forward.

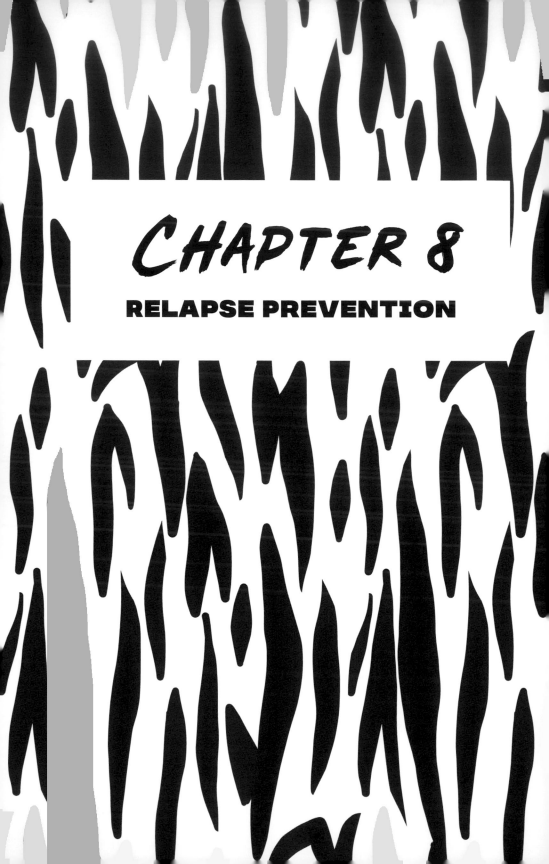

CHAPTER 8

RELAPSE PREVENTION

*T*his book aims to teach you not only how to work on the anxiety you're experiencing right now, but also how to keep that anxiety in its place in the future. If showing your anxiety your fierce side were like climbing a mountain, the top of the mountain would be you reaching your goals and doing things that you value. Climbing a mountain can be a bumpy journey, though; lapses and relapses are experiences of anxiety trying to take charge again. A lapse is like slipping while climbing and stumbling a step or so down the mountain. A relapse is tumbling back down to the base of the mountain.

For an example, let's return to Jordan, whose social anxiety made it difficult for him to attend school. Jordan worked really hard to use his skills so that he could attend school all five days each week. After he made it to that goal, he took a break from using his skills because he figured he had made it and was all set. A few weeks later, Jordan missed one day one week—a lapse. A few weeks after the lapse, Jordan started missing even more school, and eventually, he was no longer attending school any day of the week—a relapse.

When do you think it would be important for Jordan to start using his skills again? That's a trick question—it's not when you have a lapse or a relapse, it's before either happens! There is no "again" because you don't stop. It's key to keep practicing these skills on an everyday basis to keep yourself in anxiety-bossing shape. So let's talk about some strategies to help you keep up your great work and allow you to continue climbing that mountain.

An Exposure a Day Keeps the Anxiety at Bay

Practicing your anxiety skills is like brushing your teeth. If you only brushed your teeth when you got a cavity, your teeth would be full of cavities. You brush your teeth twice a day to keep the cavities away. Exposures work similarly: an exposure a day keeps the anxiety at bay. One way to help you keep your fierce fitness is to create an exposure calendar. You can plan out the exposures you aim to do for the week and then record what you learned from the experiences. Check out Emma's completed calendar for one week:

DAY	SUNDAY	MONDAY	TUESDAY	WEDNESDAY	THURSDAY	FRIDAY	SATURDAY
EXPOSURE	Smile at and make eye contact with a stranger I pass while walking my dog.	Raise my hand in science class when unsure of the answer.	Say "Good morning" to my neighbor when I walk by her on my way to school.	Raise my hand in math class and give the wrong answer.	Ask my friend at lunch to go see a movie on Saturday.	Call a restaurant and ask what time it closes.	Ask what time the movie starts at the theater, even though the start time is posted on the screen in front of me.
WHAT DID I LEARN?	I could do it!	It's OK to guess, even when I'm not sure of the answer.	I can be friendly regardless of how others respond.	My teacher did not fail me and just asked someone else for the correct answer.	I can schedule plans with friends and create an opportunity for fun.	I can make a phone call and get an answer to a question.	I can tolerate feeling embarrassed for a period of time and still enjoy a movie afterward.

EMPOWER COPING CARD

Sometimes when you're feeling anxious, your emotions can make it difficult to remember which skills to use. Because of this, you might find it helpful to carry a coping card with you to remind you of your skills. You can use EMPOWER, an acronym that can help you remember your strategies, like on the coping card example here, or you can make a card with other coping strategies that work for you. There's no right or wrong here—whatever works best for you is what's best!

If you make an EMPOWER card, you can fill in examples for each letter of the acronym if that helps you remember your tools, or you can leave it open-ended.

Exposures
When you're in a situation that makes you feel anxious and convinced that you're unable to survive the outcome, try an exposure to prove to your brain that you can do it. Some examples could be raising your hand in class, ordering in a restaurant, or sending a text message to a friend.

Mindfulness and Relaxation
Mindfulness and relaxation exercises are not the same, but both can be helpful in managing your anxiety.

Mindfulness skills keep your attention on the present moment so that your brain can learn that you can handle the experience. The skills also help you bring your focus back to the present moment and away from the future, where anxiety often tries to make life more challenging. You might write down the 5, 4, 3, 2, 1 and mindful eating exercises on your coping card.

Relaxation exercises help you loosen the tension from your body so that your brain will catch on and follow the same path to settle. Your coping card can also help remind you to use your relaxation skills an hour or so before an anticipated stressful event. Maybe you find diaphragmatic breathing and PMR helpful tools worth writing down.

Past Evidence

The present moment has been getting a lot of attention, especially with the talk about mindfulness, but there is actually a way to use your past for a skill—reminding yourself of when you have achieved something in the past can give you confidence that you can do it again. If Jordan started worrying about being embarrassed in class and then had an urge to avoid school, he could remind himself that he successfully attended full classes throughout his childhood up until this school year. He could say, "I've done it before, so I can do it again!"

For the experiences that make you worried, think about if you have made it through a similar situation in the past. If you have, you've got past evidence that you have done it before and can do it again!

OFFER A FRIEND ADVICE

We typically are less kind to ourselves than we are to others; we can be our own worst enemies and harshest critics. One way to get around this when you're feeling distressed is to imagine giving your best friend advice on how to manage the very same situation. For example, if Emma were worried that after answering a question in class her peers would think she was stupid and she would feel embarrassed forever, she could pretend to give her best friend, Lauren, advice about how to work through the anxiety. Sometimes the answers come more easily when we're not trying to apply them to ourselves. Emma might pretend to say to Lauren, "No one can read minds or feel anxious forever. Even if everyone in class did think you were stupid, then they would have room for growth for being judgmental. What would be the point of being in school if you already knew all of the answers?" After pretending to say this to Lauren, Emma can then give the same advice to herself.

WHAT IS THE WORST THAT COULD HAPPEN? COULD YOU HANDLE IT?
When you find yourself in a situation that makes you feel anxious, anxiety may try to put up a steel wall in front of you and say, "Don't even think about going in there!" Anxiety likes to convince people that a situation is dangerous and that it's not even worth thinking through what might happen if you were to approach the situation. This skill helps you say, "You know what anxiety? Let's do it your way and walk through the very worst-case scenario, so I can show you how I'd handle even the worst possible (but also not very likely) outcome!"

If Emma's anxiety tells her she can't raise her hand in class because she might give the wrong answer, she could show her anxiety who's boss by imagining what would happen in the worst-case scenario if she did give the wrong answer. What could happen?

Emma gives the wrong answer→ The teacher says, "No, that is wrong"→ Her classmates laugh and give Emma dirty looks while saying under their breaths, "What an idiot for missing that question"→ Emma feels embarrassed and blushes for a few minutes→ Emma no longer feels embarrassed because emotions don't last forever→ Her classmates move on to think about themselves/what they have for homework that night.

The outcome above would not be ideal, but could Emma handle feeling embarrassed for a few minutes? Yes. It may be uncomfortable, but Emma could realize that even the worst-case scenario would be doable. To help you figure out just how likely that worst-case scenario even would be, check out the next skill, evaluate the probability.

EVALUATE THE PROBABILITY

Anxiety likes to pretend to be a scientist, but it usually doesn't have any data for its experiments. Instead, it likes to assume the worst will happen, even though it would be very rare for the worst to happen. To put anxiety in its place, evaluate the probability that the feared outcome will actually happen.

Let's go back to Emma and her fear. If Emma were just starting her sophomore year in high school and had been in school at least since Kindergarten, for 180 school days per year, that means that she has attended about 1,800 school days (180 school days x 10 school years). Emma can ask herself, "Out of 1,800 school days, how many of those did my classmates laugh at me and say, 'What an idiot for missing that question' after I gave the wrong answer?" Emma most likely would say zero. What is zero divided by 1,800 (or by any number)? Zero. That means that there is a 0% probability that Emma's worst-case scenario will happen. Remember, you are a scientist. Scientists need data to support their hypotheses. There are no data to support the hypothesis that Emma's classmates will laugh at her and say, "What an idiot for missing that question" after she gave the wrong answer.

Think of a courtroom in which anxiety's lawyer has to provide a judge with evidence that the feared outcome will happen. A judge wouldn't waste time listening to an argument saying, "Your honor, this has not happened yet, but what if it were to happen?" The judge would send anxiety's lawyer straight out of the courtroom! Without data, you don't have a case. Ask yourself if a judge would hear this case. If the answer is no, then tell anxiety to back off!

Even if the probability is slightly more than 0% because you experienced something once or twice, remember two things: first, that the probability is still extremely low, and second, that experience is now past evidence that you handled it before and can do it again!

Reward Your Efforts

Rewarding yourself can help recharge the motivation battery that energizes your inner fierce. When you notice that it's tough to keep going, that may be a time to re-evaluate your reward list and make sure that it has rewards that motivate you. It's also a cue to make sure that you're cashing in your rewards regularly, at least twice per week, so that your motivation battery remains charged.

PUTTING IT INTO PRACTICE

"You have got to be kidding me. She wants us to do a group project? Now?! With no warning?! I can't do this. I'm going to give the wrong answer, and they're going to think I'm a useless idiot. I'll make us fail, and my group members will hate me forever!"

Jordan can use EMPOWER to encourage himself to participate in the group project. Some example EMPOWER thoughts are listed—can you think of some additional ones?

Exposures: I'll try my best during the group project to show myself that I can handle participating, even if it won't be my favorite school assignment.

Mindfulness/Relaxation: When I start to worry what my group members are thinking of me, I can use my mindfulness 5, 4, 3, 2, 1 skill.

Past evidence: Last year, I did a group project. My group and I did not fail, and my group members still talked to me after the assignment was done. If I did that then, I can do it again now.

Offer a friend advice: "Tyler, your group members are not experts either and won't know the answers to everything. Everyone is learning in class, and all of you can work together to try to tackle the assignment. Everyone has something to contribute. Plus, if your group members think you're an idiot and useless for trying your best, then they're not team players and could use some training on that!"

Worst-Case Scenario: The worst that could happen is that I give a wrong answer or suggest an idea that does not work. I can't read minds, so I wouldn't know if my group members thought I was a "useless idiot" and planned to hate me forever. If my group members actually thought I was a "useless idiot" and planned to hate me forever, then they would be missing the point of school: a place to not know everything and a place to try to learn new things! All I can do is try my best.

My group members even in the worst-case scenario probably just would tell me that I'm wrong or that the idea wouldn't work. I would feel embarrassed, but that emotion would not last forever. The group would continue working on the project, and I could try offering another idea instead. It would be uncomfortable, but I could do it!

Evaluate the probability: Out of all of the group projects that I have done in the past, there have been zero times when I got an F on the assignment, had my group members tell me that I'm a "useless idiot," or that they hated me. Zero divided by any number is zero, so there is a 0% likelihood that my worries will happen.

Reward your efforts: I am 100% going to my favorite pizza place after school!

"DEAR FUTURE ME" LETTER

Another way to cope with freezing and forgetting one's skills in the moment is to have a pre-written letter to yourself in your own words about how to find your fierce. When you are feeling relatively calm, write a letter to your future self about a specific feared situation with tips. Start off by describing how you might feel initially in the situation and then remind yourself of strategies you can use in the moment to help you approach the feared situation. Check out Emma's letter to her future self as an example:

Dear Future Me,

Today, you will wake up with butterflies in your stomach, think to yourself, "Everyone will call me 'stupid' or think I'm stupid if I say the wrong answer in class," and you'll have the urge to pull your covers over your head and hide. Remember to channel your inner scientist by reminding yourself that you cannot read minds. Also, out of the 1,800 days you have been to school so far, no one ever has said you were stupid for giving the wrong answer in class, so the probability of that happening today is 0%. You don't have any data to prove that will happen.

And even if it did happen, that would mean that your classmates have some serious room for growth and have not gotten the memo that school is for learning.

Keep your mind on the present moment and not on what you're worried will happen in the future. Practice your 5, 4, 3, 2, 1 skill. Keep your eyes on the prize of going to school, seeing your best friend Lauren, and picking what you want for dinner tonight as a reward. You've got this!

Love,

Past Me

The "Dear Future Me" letter is another way to have your skills at your fingertips. After you write your letter, keep it in your pocket, wallet, backpack, or another place where you will have quick access to it.

AHEAD OF THE GAME PLAN

Anxiety spends a lot of time making you worry about the future and making you feel stuck. Creating an "Ahead of the Game Plan" helps you get ahead of anxiety by thinking through how you might handle future challenging situations. Instead of stewing over whether the situations might happen, match your anxiety's catastrophic thinking with a plan to help you cope with those potential situations if they were to come your way.

If you suspect that situations that make you feel anxious—such as going to a birthday party, having a speech to present, or getting called on in class—may happen in the near future, complete an Ahead of the Game Plan for each scenario to help you approach each situation. Check out Maria's example chart below, and then try making one for yourself. The first few questions will help you anticipate what you might experience. Then a question about your relevant values is there to remind you what's important to you and help motivate you to approach the situation. The final question encourages you to select skills that you could use in that situation to help you have a value-driven experience.

QUESTION	ANSWER
What is the situation?	Going to my friend's birthday dinner party
What emotion(s) would I experience?	Anxiety
What would I be thinking?	Everything I will say will sound awkward
What physical sensations would I have?	Racing heart, sweaty palms, and blushing cheeks
What unhelpful urges might I have?	I'll want to tell my friend that I am sick and cannot go to the birthday party
What are my relevant values?	I want to support my friends and connect with others
What skills could I use instead?	Stop, drop, and roll; mindful eating; and offering a friend advice

You cannot predict the future or anticipate every possible hypothetical or "What if" situation, but you can pick a few situations to help you practice your coping skills. Answer the set of questions above for each selected situation that you expect to happen soon.

USE IT OR LOSE IT

Your fierce fitness comes from repeated skill rehearsal. You are mastering the skillset of keeping your anxiety in check, and that takes work. You are not alone—even professional athletes have to practice year-round to keep in shape! If you went to the gym one day and lifted weights, would you be set for life? No. You have to keep lifting weights to maintain and increase your strength. The same goes for learning a foreign language: if you don't use it, you lose it. You might find that you have trouble remembering certain words if you don't practice. Just like athletes and foreign language speakers, practicing exposures and coping skills will keep you in anxiety-bossing shape. If you keep using your skills, then you won't lose them.

In a Nutshell

You've got a toolkit to keep up your fierce fitness and keep your anxiety in check.

* Plan for at least one exposure a day to keep anxiety at bay.

* Create a coping card using the EMPOWER acronym or your own list of helpful coping strategies to help get you through feared situations.

* Write a letter to your future self, and create an Ahead of the Game Plan to prepare for future anxiety-inducing situations.

The next chapter will teach you how to be the boss of all of your emotions, and not just your anxiety, moving forward.

CHAPTER 9

SELF-CARE

*J*ust as it's important to practice skills on a daily basis to keep your anxiety at bay, it's also key to practice daily self-care to help you manage all of your emotions, not just anxiety. In this chapter, we'll talk about some tools to help you keep all your feelings in check and you in the driver's seat of your sports car.

FUN ACTIVITIES

You may not think so at first, but participating in activities you enjoy each day is a skill, because it gives you opportunities to experience happiness. Sometimes our emotions, like sadness or anxiety, may pull us to spend time alone and lying down. Isolation and inactivity are like avoidance and are ingredients for cooking up a low mood; they can keep you from having positive experiences. It may take some extra work to collect the energy you need to resist the urge to withdraw and lay low. One way to get ahead of that is by encouraging yourself to do something you enjoy each day, regardless of your energy level. Invite company to join you when possible, so you can share some of the experiences together. Even if you do something super simple alone, that's still better than doing nothing!

Here's a list of some possible activities; feel free to make your own list of ones you enjoy.

DRAWING	PLAYING TENNIS
COOKING	HIKING
PLAYING SOCCER	ICE SKATING
GARDENING	PETTING AN ANIMAL
PAINTING	CAMPING
LISTENING TO MUSIC	THROWING A FRISBEE
READING	VOLUNTEERING
PLAYING BASKETBALL	PAINTING NAILS
CALLING A FRIEND	KAYAKING
SWIMMING	BOWLING
PLAYING BASEBALL OR CATCH	RIDING A HORSE
DOING A CROSSWORD	STAR GAZING
PLAYING AN INSTRUMENT	DOING ARCHERY
SINGING	MAKING POTTERY
DANCING	DOING GYMNASTICS
DOING A PUZZLE	PICNICKING
TAKING PICTURES	MEDITATING
BAKING	PLAYING FOOTBALL
RIDING A BICYCLE	DOING YOGA
ROLLERBLADING	FISHING
FLYING A KITE	PLAYING VOLLEYBALL
CLIMBING	WRESTLING
DOING KARATE	GOLFING
PLAYING A CARD GAME	SAILING
THROWING DARTS	

BEHAVIORAL EXPERIMENT

When you're in a funk, it can be tough to imagine how an activity would make you feel better. In these moments, it can be helpful to channel your inner scientist by conducting a behavioral experiment to see if the activities actually could have a positive impact on your mood.

Start with one week. For the first half of the week, rate your emotions at a selected time of day, such as at 3:00 p.m., on a scale from 0 to 10 (for example, sad at a 5 and anxious at a 6). Do nothing by yourself for 30 minutes. Rate your emotions again after 30 minutes, and see if it has changed at all. For the second half of the week, rate your emotions at 3:00 p.m, but then spend 30 minutes doing a fun activity from your list. After half an hour, rate your emotions again. What did you notice? Did you feel a little better after doing something fun rather than just doing nothing? If so, then you have data that doing something you enjoy each day helps your mood. You can create a chart, like Maria's on the next page, to keep track of the data you collect.

DAY, TIME	ACTIVITY OR NO ACTIVITY?	EMOTION RATINGS BEFORE	EMOTION RATINGS AFTER
Sunday, 3-3:30p.m.	No activity	Anxious (5) Sad (4)	Anxious (6) Sad (5)
Monday, 3-3:30p.m.	No activity	Anxious (6) Angry (3)	Anxious (7) Angry (5)
Tuesday, 3-3:30p.m.	No activity	Sad (4) Anxious (3)	Sad (5) Anxious (4)
Wednesday, 3-3:30p.m.	Rode my bike for 30 minutes	Anxious (5) Sad (4)	Anxious (3) Sad (2)
Thursday, 3-3:30p.m.	Rode my bike for 30 minutes	Anxious (6) Angry (3)	Anxious (2) Angry (1)
Friday, 3-3:30p.m.	Rode my bike for 30 minutes	Sad (4) Anxious (3)	Sad (2) Anxious (2)
Saturday, 3-3:30p.m.	Rode my bike for 30 minutes	Anxious (5) Sad (6) Angry (4)	Anxious (3) Sad (3) Angry (2)

Maria's mood became more intense after doing nothing for 30 minutes. On the days when Maria rode her bicycle for 30 minutes, however, Maria rated that her mood was less intense after the 30-minute ride. Maria proved to herself that engaging in a fun activity could help her manage her mood.

It can be helpful to schedule a block of time for an enjoyable activity each day to keep your feelings in check. If 30 minutes is too big a chunk of time, then make it smaller—remember, any is better than none! Try to schedule as large of a window of time as you can each day.

Some people worry that they will not have time to do other things they need to do if they make time for self-care. You could try another behavioral experiment to test that out. See if blocking off time for self-care might give you more energy and resources to do other things.

When you are in that funk in the future and thinking that you're not in the mood to do an activity, or that no activity will boost your mood, try a behavioral experiment. The only way to know for sure is to test the thoughts. Seeing is believing, and you might surprise yourself by feeling better!

BEING ACTIVE

Not only can spending time each day doing something you enjoy help you manage your emotions, but being active can, too. Making time for an activity that gets your heartrate up can boost your mood. Schedule a block of time each day for physical activity to keep you in emotion-management shape. The physical activity block can be in addition to a less physical fun activity (like reading or doing a puzzle) you have scheduled, or, if you don't have time for both, then you can pick one activity that fits into both categories, like playing a sport.

Remember, if you have doubts about whether physical activity can really boost your mood, try doing another experiment. Keep in mind that it may take a few experiments with different physical activities to find one that keeps your emotions in check—and the experiment will work better if you pick a physical activity that you enjoy instead of one that feels like a chore.

DAILY ROUTINES

We tend to be more vulnerable to our emotions bossing us around when our batteries are drained. Think about that sports car we talked about in the first chapter. It needs gas in its tank to drive. You don't want to wait until the gas tank is completely empty and the car has stalled on the highway to refill it; you want to make sure that there's always gas in the tank so the car can keep driving. The same goes for your body. For example, your hunger levels can affect your mood; you might have felt "hangry" (hungry and angry) or what I call "hanxious" (hungry and anxious) when you haven't eaten in a bit. You might find that you are more on-edge and likelier to lash out at someone when hangry and more likely to avoid when hanxious. Try to eat meals and snacks regularly to help keep yourself in charge of your emotions.

The types of foods you eat can also play a role in your mood. For example, foods rich in zinc, B vitamins, and omega-3 fatty acids have been linked to reducing anxiety. It might be helpful to speak with your doctor first to learn about healthy food choices that may be best for you before making any drastic changes to your diet, but in general, eating a balanced and healthy diet is going to help keep your tank full.

Healthy sleep hygiene is another way to keep fuel in your tank and you in charge of your emotions. When you don't get enough sleep, emotions try to take the wheel. Poor sleep can interfere not only with your mental health but also with your physical health and performance in school. Establishing healthy sleep habits can help you have more restful sleep, which gives you more resources to make your days more manageable.

Getting regular sleep is easier said than done, but there are ways to make it a little more doable.

Keep a Consistent Schedule

It can be so tempting to sleep in on the weekends when you're tired from the school week. Unfortunately, the change in sleep schedule can come back to bite you. If you sleep in an extra four hours on Sunday, what do you think will happen when you try to go to bed that night? You'd probably have a hard time falling asleep early enough to wake up in time for school the next day, and then you'd be exhausted Monday morning. That would be a very rough way to start the week. Instead, try to keep your bedtime and wake-up times as consistent as possible each day of the week for more restful sleep and more energy to approach the next day.

Stop Screen Use Before Bed

Brains release melatonin, a hormone that helps you fall asleep. Any device with a blue light-emitting screen, such as a phone, tablet, or computer, tells the brain to stop releasing melatonin and to stay awake instead. In addition to the light from the screen, the activity you do while using the screen also can keep the brain awake. Allowing your brain at least 30 minutes away from screens before bed can help it prepare your body to go to sleep.

Unwind Before Bed

After you turn off your screens is a good time to start doing low-key activities that don't rev up your sports car's engine or energize your brain. For example, this can be a good time to start brushing your teeth, washing your face, reading, etc.

Use the Bed Only for Sleeping

Your brain is a super-sharp learner and will pick up on patterns it notices. This happens with activities your brain observes you doing while in your bed. If you watch TV, talk on the phone, or do homework while sitting on your bed, your brain will think that it's a place where it should stay awake. Because of this pattern-making skill, your brain may then keep you awake when you're trying to fall asleep in your bed. If you use your bed only for sleeping, your brain will learn that it needs to sleep instead of to stay awake when you're there.

SELF-COMPASSION

In addition to daily routines, self-compassion, or being kind to and understanding of yourself, can shield you from distress. We are often our own harshest critics, so this skill is easier said than done and will take practice. There are three steps to help you exercise self-compassion.

SELF-KINDNESS

Beating yourself up about what has happened in the past is like using one of the unhelpful thoughts from Chapter 3, "Shoulds and Musts." "I shouldn't have said that" won't change what already happened, and criticizing yourself about what you did will probably just make you feel worse. Instead, try practicing some kindness in the moment. Maybe you could say, "I can't change the past, but I can try to say something different in a similar situation in the future."

You may worry that self-compassion is a way to let yourself off the hook and get away with what happened. In this case, however, you're aiming to try to behave differently in the future. Punishing yourself does not change the past and does not help your future. Offering kindness and understanding to yourself may create some space and motivation to behave differently next time.

COMMON HUMANITY

Remind yourself that everyone makes mistakes and has room for growth. There is no such thing as perfect. Practice does not make perfect; practice makes progress.

MINDFULNESS

Mindfulness is back! Practice noticing your thoughts without judging them. Noticing instead of judging the thoughts can create some distance between you and your thoughts; it might make them feel less in your face. Judging your thoughts, on the other hand, would be like pressing the thoughts right up against your face.

To practice mindfulness, you might say to yourself, "I notice that I'm having the thought, 'I shouldn't have said that,'" and then place that thought on an imaginary lily pad that is floating along an imaginary river. Watch the thought and lily pad float away. Next, gently bring your mind back to the present moment, and focus on what is going on around you. Use all your senses while leaving the judgments behind. If you notice some judgments cropping back up, place them on lily pads and let them float away.

Another way to use mindfulness for self-compassion is to focus on the emotions you are experiencing in the present moment. Acknowledge how you're feeling without judging yourself for having that feeling. For example, you might say, "I'm feeling embarrassed and frustrated right now." Telling yourself, "I should not feel embarrassed or frustrated" would be a judgment. Acknowledging how you feel without judging yourself for it can help you manage your feelings.

PUTTING IT INTO PRACTICE

Jordan's down on himself and is thinking about quitting soccer again. He can apply self-compassion by coming up with some phrases and activities he can use to keep him on the field and doing what he loves. He might say:

"I didn't do that on purpose. I tried my best, and no goalie blocks every shot. I haven't played in a while either, so practicing more after school might help me do better in future games."

Noticing that he tried his best is practicing self-kindness; realizing that no goalie blocks every shot is an example of noticing common humanity.

Jordan could also practice mindfulness by using all his senses to keep him grounded in the moment when he notices unkind thoughts popping up.

Sight: Observe all the colors on the soccer jerseys, the cleats, the field, and the goals.

Smell: Notice the scents of the fresh breeze and recently mowed grass.

Taste: Taste the lingering tangy flavor of the orange slice he ate during half-time.

Touch: Focus on the texture of the mouth guard or goalie gloves he is wearing.

Hear: Notice the sounds of his teammates running across the field and families cheering on the players.

BUILDING MASTERY

When anxiety spends a lot of time trying to convince you that you'll be embarrassed or judged by talking to others, performing, or going out in public, it can be common to have low self-esteem and lack confidence in your ability to do anything well. Another way to boss back the anxiety is by building a sense of mastery in different areas of your life to give your self-esteem reminders that you can do a variety of activities.

Where do you even begin? Think about any activities that you enjoy that don't necessarily have a performance element, so that you can focus on the process versus the outcome. You also might consider activities that help others—some people find that helping others boosts their own well-being in the process. For example, you might volunteer at a community center, babysit, clean a room that's not yours at home, or take care of a neighbor's animal when the neighbor is away.

MONITORING MASTERY

Pick one activity to do each week, and notice how you feel afterward. On a separate piece of paper, you can create a chart like the one on the next page to help you keep track of your efforts. Rate how you feel before and after doing the activity, including how proud you are of yourself as one of the emotions, to see if the ratings change afterward. While you are working hard to put anxiety in its place, these mastery-building experiences can remind you that you have a lot to offer and can make a positive impact just by being you.

THIS WEEK I HELPED SOMEONE BY...	BEFORE EMOTION RATING(S) (0–10 SCALE)	AFTER EMOTION RATINGS(S) (0–10 SCALE)
Learning how to garden and planting flowers for my neighbor's yard	Worried (4) Sad (3) Happy (2) Proud (1)	Worried (2) Sad (1) Happy (4) Proud (5)

IN A NUTSHELL

Taking care of yourself each day will refuel your car's gas tank and help keep your social anxiety out of the driver's seat. Although it's important to practice exposures and skills each day to make sure that your social anxiety remains in check, continuing your self-care routine each day is key to providing you with the resources to approach the brave work.

* Take care of your body's physical needs by doing fun activities, eating well, and getting good sleep.

* Practice self-compassion by being kind to yourself, noticing common humanity, and using mindfulness.

* Build mastery in another area to boost self-esteem.

So, what's next?

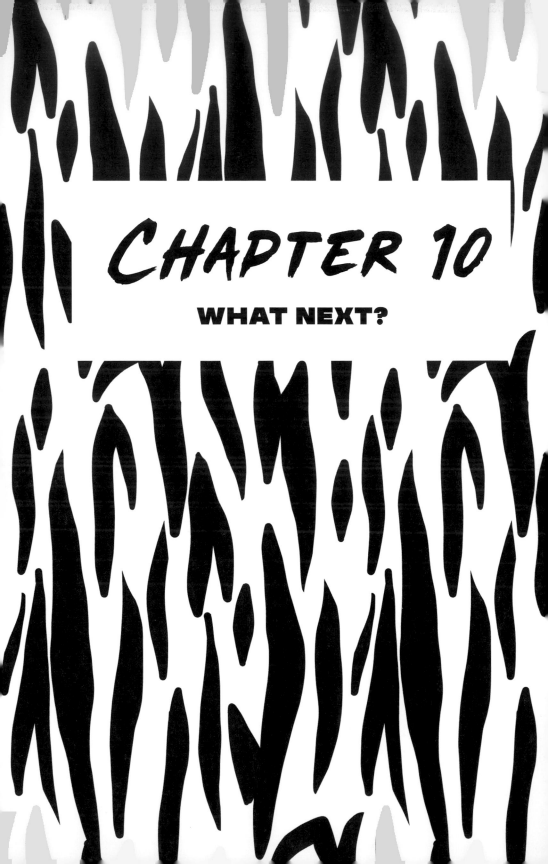

CHAPTER 10

WHAT NEXT?

*N*ow that you've read the driver's manual for your sports car, it's time to take it out for a test drive. Come up with a daily skill-rehearsal plan that is feasible for you. Some find it helpful to make a schedule for each day. For example, maybe you will include mindfulness when you're getting ready for school, complete a few social anxiety exposures while at school, use "Stop, Drop, and Roll" before starting your homework, and do relaxation strategies before going to bed. Remember, these skills take practice, and so does learning how to navigate the roads with your car. You deserve the time to practice now so you can zoom ahead to where you want to go in the future.

Keep in mind that the road to improvement is not smooth; it's a bumpy path that will include days that may feel more challenging than others. Remember that you're not back at the beginning on any of those rough days; you've hit a bump in the road that may require some extra practice for you to move ahead. You're still moving forward.

By approaching your fears, you will open doors to new opportunities. New experiences will bring unfamiliarity and uncertainty, and that's to be expected. No one shows up to a new experience knowing how to do it fully. Give yourself multiple opportunities to learn in each new experience so that your brain can realize that, with practice, you've got what it takes to make the most of the situation.

PRACTICE MAKES PROGRESS

You might be wondering what a road to improvement could look like for someone with social anxiety. Everyone's path will be a bit different, but by using the skills learned in this book, there can be a trend of practice making progress. Below are examples of what Emma's, Jordan's, and Maria's experiences have been like after using skills from this book:

EMMA used to avoid ordering in restaurants, seeking help from a teacher, raising her hand in class, eating in the cafeteria, and asking people questions. Now, she has started eating lunch with her close friends in the cafeteria at school. She can also eat dinner at her favorite restaurant with her family. She's working her way up to going to the most popular restaurant in town that serves messy food, like corn on the cob. She also recently started raising her hand in class, and her grades have been improving because of that.

Emma's anxiety made it difficult to perform the way she would have liked during her audition for the lead role in the school play, but after reminding herself that experiences take practice, she earned the second biggest role in the play after coming back and nailing the next round of auditions.

Emma also just said "Yes" to going to the school dance with her crush, which will be one of her biggest exposure challenges ever! She's nervous about appearing awkward while dancing in front of others, so she made a plan to do some overlearning beforehand by making goofy dance moves randomly when she's at a store. Emma reminds herself that even though she may be uncomfortable at times, she's appreciating getting to spend more time with her friends and family by doing exposures.

JORDAN had stopped attending soccer practices and games, quit playing the piano, avoided raising his hand in class when he wasn't sure of the answer, and skipped school on days when group projects or speeches were involved. Now, after trying out for and making the town's soccer team, he has attended every practice and game of the season so far. He had an urge to skip a game after an opposing team's player cheered when Jordan missed blocking a goal, but Jordan reminded himself that not even the pros block every shot. Jordan aims to practice with the town team so he can work up the courage to try out for the travel team next season.

Jordan was disappointed to have to take summer school classes to make up the work his missed due to his anxiety, but he decided to make the most of the experience by practicing raising his hand even when he was not sure of the answer.

Jordan also started playing the piano again and recently added using the pedals while playing the piano keys. A couple performances ago, Jordan stepped on the pedal at the wrong time. He felt really embarrassed, turned bright red, and froze for the remainder of the recital. He wanted to quit playing after that, but after reminding himself of his values and that new experiences take work to iron out the kinks, Jordan decided to go to his next recital after all. Jordan played some notes at the wrong time, but it was better than the last performance—because he kept playing even after he made some mistakes. Jordan realized that feeling more confident while playing the piano would take time, so he decided to teach soccer dribbling skills to elementary school-aged children to help others, create opportunities for mastery, and feel proud of himself.

MARIA had trouble making eye contact, starting conversations, going to public places where she might run into her peers, and attending birthday parties. Now, she makes sure to look straight ahead while using mindfulness when she walks down the school hallways. She challenges herself to start one new conversation each day, and she's working up to starting a conversation with a student she doesn't know to help her prepare for an upcoming birthday party of a classmate she doesn't know very well.

Maria recently noticed herself avoiding texting Sophie after sending a message with a typo. After reminding herself that everyone makes mistakes, she decided to reach out to Sophie to see how her weekend was going. Sophie responded by inviting Maria to go see a movie. Going to a movie is a big exposure for Maria, but she was excited that reaching back out allowed her to spend more time with her friend. Now Maria and Sophie try to go see a movie together every couple of weeks, and Maria rewards her brave efforts by getting popcorn, her favorite movie-viewing snack. Maria has also practiced advocating for herself by asking Sophie if she wants to see movies that interest Maria and not just agreeing to see whichever movie Sophie picks.

GETTING EXTRA HELP

Sometimes, even with repeated practice of skills, you might find that you're getting stuck more often than not. If that happens, you're not alone, and there are additional resources to help you do what's important to you. Below are some options for extra support.

COGNITIVE BEHAVIORAL THERAPY (CBT)

Finding your fierce and putting social anxiety in its place takes work, and sometimes, it can be helpful to seek extra support from a mental health clinician who provides CBT to guide you. Even professional athletes have coaches to help them practice their skills, so you would not be alone in getting tips from an expert. You would be taking driving lessons to learn how to drive the sports car before heading out on the roads by yourself. You don't have to do this alone. Know that you have this book, and there are mental health clinicians if you need them.

MEDICATION

Medication is another treatment that may help when social anxiety is getting in the way of daily life. A type of medication called selective serotonin reuptake inhibitors (SSRIs) has been shown to be helpful for youth with social anxiety, and the combination of CBT and SSRIs can be even more helpful for youth anxiety than either CBT or SSRIs individually. Medical professionals like psychiatrists and pediatricians can help decide whether medication might be helpful for you.

FIND YOUR FIERCE

Your fierce will never leave you; sometimes, you just need to find it before you can channel it. Remind yourself when you hit a bump in the road that you have what it takes to keep driving. You've got this!

AFTERWORD

I am tremendously thankful for the support of my family, friends, and colleagues as this book would not have been possible without it. I also am indebted to my mentors, who believed in, encouraged, and shared their knowledge with me. In addition, I am grateful for the families with whom I have the privilege to work. Their courage, willingness, commitment, and perseverance inspire me each day.

REFERENCES

American Academy of Pediatrics. (2016). *American Academy of Pediatrics supports childhood sleep guidelines.* https://www.aap.org/en-us/about-the-aap/aap-press-room/Pages/American-Academy-of-Pediatrics-Supports-Childhood-Sleep-Guidelines.aspx.

Anxiety and Depression Association of America. (n.d.). Symptoms. Retrieved from: https://adaa.org/understanding-anxiety/panic-disorder-agoraphobia/symptoms.

Benito, K. G., & Walther, M. (2015). Therapeutic process during exposure: Habituation model. *Journal of Obsessive-Compulsive and Related Disorders, 6,* 147-157. doi.org/10.1016/j.jocrd.2015.01.006.

Brown, H. E. Pearson, N., Braithwaite, R. E., Brown, W. J., & Biddle, S. J. H. (2013). Physical activity interventions and depression in children and adolescents: A systematic review and meta-analysis. *Sports Medicine, 43(3),* 195-206. doi.org/10.1007/s40279012-0015-8.

Brown, T. A., LeBeau, R., Liao, B., Niles, A. N., Glenn, D., & Craske, M. G. (2016). A comparison of the nature and correlates of panic attacks in the context of panic disorder and social anxiety disorder. *Psychiatry Research, 235 (30),* 69-76,

Bowles, T. (2016). The focus of intervention for adolescent social anxiety: Communication skills or self-esteem. *International Journal of School & Educational Psychology, 5(1),* 14-25. doi.org/10.1080/21683603.2016.1157051.

Buxton, O. R., Chang, A., Spilsbury, J. C., Bos, T., Emsellem, H., & Knutson, K. L. (2015). Sleep in the modern family: Protective family routines for child and adolescent sleep. *Sleep Health, 1(1),* 15-27. doi.org/10.1016/j.sleh.2014.12.002.

Craske, M. G., Treanor, M., Conway, C. C., Zbozinek, T., & Vervliet, B. (2014). Maximizing exposure therapy: An inhibitory learning approach. *Behaviour Research and Therapy, 58,* 10-23. doi.org/10.1016/j.brat.2014.04.006.

Curry, O. S., Rowland, L. A., Van Lissa, C. J., Zlotowitz, S., McAlaney, J., & Whitehouse, H. (2018). Happy to help? A systematic review and meta-analysis of the effects of performing acts of kindness on the well-being of the actor. *Journal of Experimental Social Psychology, 76,* 320-329. doi.org/10.1016/j.jesp.2018.02.014.

Gotter, A. (2019, February 22). *Box breathing.* Healthline. https://www.healthline.com/health/box-breathing#slowly-exhale.

Higa-McMillan, C. K., Francis, S. E., Rith-Najarian, L., & Chorpita, B. F. (2016). Evidence base update: 50 years of research on treatment for child and adolescent anxiety. *Journal of Clinical Child and Adolescent Psychology, 45*(2), 91-113. doi.org/10.1080/15374416.2015.1046177.

Horman, T., Fernandes, M.F., Zhou, Y., Fuller, B., Tigert, M., & Leri, F. (2018). An exploration of the aversive properties of 2-deoxy-D-glucose in rats. *Psychopharmacology, 235*(10), 3055-2063. doi.org/10.1007/s00213-018-4998-1.

Hyde, J., Ryan, K. M., & Waters, A. M. (2019). Psychophysiological markers of fear and anxiety. *Current Psychiatry Reports, 21*, 56-66. doi.org/10.1007/s11920-019-1035-x.

Jacobson, E. (1938). *Progressive relaxation.* University of Chicago Press.

Kabat-Zinn, J. (1994). *Mindfulness meditation for everyday life.* Hyperion.

Keltner D., & Ekman P. (2003). Introduction: Expression of emotion. In R.J. Davidson & K.R. Scherer (Eds.), *Handbook of affective sciences* (411-414). Oxford University Press.

Ma, X., Yu, Z., Gong, Z., Zhang, H., Duan, N., Shi, Y.,...& Li, Y. (2017). The effect of Diaphragmatic breathing on attention, negative affect, and stress in healthy adults. *Frontiers in Psychology, 8*, 874-876. doi.org/10.3389/fpsyg.2017.00874.

Mazzucchelli, T. G., Kane, R. T., & Rees, C. S. (2010). Behavioral activation interventions for well-being: A meta-analysis. *The Journal of Positive Psychology, 5*(2), 105-121. doi.org/10.1080/17439760903569154.

Merikangas, K. R., He, J. P., Burstein, M., Swanson, S. A., Avenevoli, S., Cui, L.,...Swendsen J. (2010). Lifetime prevalence of mental disorders in U.S. adolescents: results from the National Comorbidity Survey Replication—Adolescent Supplement (NCS-A). *Journal of the American Academy of Child & Adolescent Psychiatry, 49*(10), 980-9. doi.org/10.1016/j.jaac.2010.05.017.

Muris, P. (2016). A protective factor against mental health factors in youth? A critical note on the assessment of self-compassion. *Journal of Child and Family Studies, 25*(5), 1461-1465. doi.org/10.1007/s10826-015-0315-3.

Naidoo, U. (2016, April 13). *Nutritional strategies to ease anxiety*. Harvard Health Publishing. https://www.health.harvard.edu/blog/nutritional-strategies-to-ease-anxiety-201604139441.

Neff, K. D. (2003). Self-compassion: An alternative conceptualization of a healthy attitude toward oneself. *Self and Identity, 2*, 85–101. doi.org/10.1080/15298860309032.

Nesse, R., Bhatnagar, S., & Ellis, B. (2016). Evolutionary origins and functions ofthe stress response system. In G. Fink (Ed.), *Stress: Concepts, cognition, emotion, and behavior* (pp. 95-101). Academic Press.

O'Neil, A., Quirk, S. E., Houdsen, S., Brennan, S. L., William, L. J., Pasco, J. A.,...Jacka, F. N. (2014). Relationship between diet and mental health in children and adolescents: A systematic review. *The American Journal of Public Health, 104*(10), 31-42. doi.org/10.2105/AJPH.2014.302110.

Segool, N. K., & Carlson, J. S. (2008). Efficacy of cognitive-behavioral and pharmacological treatments for children with social anxiety. *Depression and Anxiety, 25*(7), 620-631. doi.org/10.1002/da.20410.

Spitzmuller, M., & Van Dyne, L. (2013). Proactive and reactive helping: Contrasting the positive consequences of different forms of helping. *Journal of Organizational Behavior, 34*, 560-580. doi.org/10.1002/job.1848.

Stanford Children's Health. (n.d.). *Healthy Eating During Adolescence.* https://www.stanfordchildrens.org/en/topic/default?id=healthy-eating-during-adolescence-90-P01610.

Steimer, T. (2002). The biology of fear- and anxiety-related behaviors. *Dialogues in Clinical Neuroscience, 4*(3), 231-249.

Stein, M. B., Chen, C. Y., Jain, S., Jensen, K. P., He, F., Heeringa, S. G., ... Army STARRS Collaborators. (2017). Genetic risk variants for social anxiety. *American Journal of Medical Genetics Part B: Neuropsychiatric Genetics, 174*(2), 120–131. doi.org/10.1002/ajmg.b.32520.

Wang, Z., Whiteside, S. P. H., Sim, L., Farah, W., Morrow, A. S., Alsawas, M.,...Murad, M. H. (2017). Comparative effectiveness and safety of cognitive behavioral therapy and pharmacotherapy for childhood anxiety disorders: A systematic review and meta-analysis. *JAMA Pediatrics, 171*(11), 1049-1056. doi.org/10.1001/jamapediatrics.2017.3036.

Yemm, G. (2012). *Essential guide to leading your team: How to set goals, measurable performance, and reward talent.* Pearson Education Limited.

Zoogman, S., Goldberg, S. B., Hoyt, W. T., & Miller, L. (2015). Mindfulness interventions with youth: A meta-analysis. *Mindfulness, 6*(2), 290-302. doi.org/10.1007/s12671-013-0260-4.

INDEX

E

Emma example
continuing exposures in, 104–105
Dear Future Me letter in, 115
evaluate the probability in, 110–111
evaluating exposures in, 91
fear-facing ladder in, 77–78
identifying emotions in, 21
mindful eating in, 50–51
offer a friend advice in, 108
overview of, 6
progress in, 138–139
reward system in, 98
what is the worst that could happen? in, 109–110
Emotional reasoning (unhelpful thought), 34, 37
Emotions, 17–25
and fun activities, 121, 123–125, 134
identifying, 17–22, 94
and the mind and body connection, 22–25
noticing without judging, 131–132
tracking thoughts, behaviors, and, 30–31
EMPOWER coping card, 105–114
Environment, changing in exposures, 94
Evaluate the probability (coping strategy), 110–111
Exposure and response prevention (ERP), 71–87
based on inhibitory learning model, 73–74
in cognitive behavioral therapy, 9
fear-facing ladder in, 77–83
and overlearning, 75–77
and safety behaviors, 84–86

Subjective Units of Distress Scale in, 72–73
Exposures, 89–101
combining, 93–94
continuing, for relapse prevention, 104–105
as coping strategy, 106
in exposure and response prevention, 71
how to do, 89–91
maximizing learning from, 93–96
preparing for, 99–100
rewards for, 96–99
tracking, 92–93

F

Fear
benefits of approaching, 137–138
identifying, 18–19
of judgment or embarrassment, 5
using relaxation exercises before activities that cause, 67
Fear-facing ladder, 77–83
Feelings, 29–31. See also Emotions
Fight-or-flight system, 22–23
5,4,3,2,1 exercise, 51–52
Focusing on the negative (unhelpful thought), 33, 37
Fun activities, 121–125

G

Goals
in building fear-facing ladders, 82–83
setting, 11–15

JACQUELINE SPERLING, PHD, is a clinical psychologist, faculty at Harvard Medical School, and the co-founder of and the Director of Training and Research at the McLean Anxiety Mastery Program at McLean Hospital. Dr. Sperling specializes in implementing evidence-based treatments, such as cognitive behavioral therapy, and working with youth who present with anxiety disorders and/or obsessive-compulsive disorder. She also focuses on providing parent guidance by using treatments, such as behavioral parent training, to help families address children's internalizing and externalizing behaviors.

ANYA KUVARZINA graduated from Central Saint Martins College of Art and Design and earned her MA from Goldsmiths University. She blogs about illustration on YouTube and Instagram. She lives in London, UK. Visit treesforanya.com, @TreesForAnya on Facebook and Twitter, and @anyakuvarzina on Pinterest.

MAGINATION PRESS is the children's book imprint of the American Psychological Association. APA works to advance psychology as a science and profession and as a means of promoting health and human welfare. Magination Press books reach young readers and their parents and caregivers to make navigating life's challenges a little easier. It's the combined power of psychology and literature that makes a Magination Press book special. Visit maginationpress.org and @MaginationPress on Facebook, Twitter, Instagram, and Pinterest.